THE
WEST END
Mismanagement and Snobbery

First Published 1983
Copyright © John Pick 1983

ISBN 0 903931 54 0

CITY ARTS SERIES
General Editor: John Pick

John Offord (Publications) Ltd.
PO Box 64, Eastbourne, East Sussex.

Book Design: John Offord
Printed by Cooper Harvey Ltd.

2

The popular humours of a great city are a never-failing source of amusement to the man whose sympathies are hospitable enough to embrace all his kind, and who, refined though he may be himself, will not sneer at the humble wit or the grotesque peculiarities of the boozing mechanic, the squalid beggar, the vicious urchin, and all the motley group of the idle, the reckless, and the imitative that swarm in the alleys and broadways of a metropolis.

Charles Mackay Ll.D.
Extraordinary Popular Delusions and the Madness of Crowds
1841

to
John and Jenny

Contents

Illustrations

The author acknowledges with thanks permission to quote from *The Noël Coward Diaries* (edited by Graham Payn and Sheridan Morley), published by Little, Brown and Company, Boston and Toronto, and the help received from staff at the Museum of London and the Victoria and Albert Museum's Enthoven Collection.

Preface

This book is a history of the growth of the West End theatre. It is inevitably also an account of the growth of British theatre management over the last hundred years, for in that time the aims and practices of theatre management in general have been largely dominated by the aims and practices of the London theatrical establishment.

I have used the terms 'management' and 'manager' as generously as the Society of West End Theatre does:

> 'All proprietors, lessees, licensees, tenants and managers of West End of London theatres and all proprietors and managers of Producing Companies producing plays in the West End of London shall at the discretion of the Executive Committee be eligible for membership subject as hereinafter provided. The expression 'Manager' shall be deemed to include the Chairman, Managing Director, Director or Officer of a limited liability company otherwise eligible.'
> *SWET Rules and Regulations*

Equally I have not tried to impose any new sociological or geographical definition of that notoriously difficult term 'West End'. I hope that the nature of 'West End management' will emerge clearly enough from the historical account, without any attempt being made to analyse it in alien terms.

In one area however we cannot avoid consistent difficulty. Money has to be talked about, but any historical account faces the twin difficulty of our having both changed our coinage, and suffered inflation so severe as to render costs and prices of even thirty years ago virtually meaningless. When we learn that Beerbohm Tree was lured into films by a four figure fee we do not know whether he was paid a fortune, or didn't know his real market price. We simply cannot grasp what a thousand pounds *meant* before the first World War.

We can at least lessen the first difficulty by reminding ourselves of our childhood tables:

Twelve pennies make one shilling. 12d. = 1s. (or 1/-)
Twenty shillings make one pound. 20/- = £1

And the second difficulty can be at least brought within tolerable bounds by reminding ourselves from time to time of what was the average wage, and what other things could be bought for the price of a theatre stall.

For their help, and for the inspiration of their writings I am most grateful to Professor Michael J. Booth and to Professor John Allen. For many illuminating conversations I should like to thank in particular Simon Trussler, Dr Michael Hammet and Dr Robert Protherough. For their help in finding material I must also record a debt to Freda Steel, Ivor Davies, Jane Purkiss, Ian Saville, James Parker and those many people working in the West End who have helped with material - some of it altogether too inflammatory for print, but all of it helpful in presenting the picture of the theatrical establishment at work. At various times I have leaned heavily upon the work of Diana Howard, Ernest Short and Jim Hiley, and for other courtesies I am indebted to Vincent Burke, Peter Hepple and Michael Quine.

To that most enterprising and courteous of publishers, John Offord, we all continue to offer our gratitude, not least because in spite of all the bureaucracy and the snobbery, he still believes the theatre can be fun.

John Pick
City University

1
Mismanagement and Snobbery

Do not wonder, but consider, that tho' the Town was then, perhaps, not much more than half so Populous as now, yet then the Prices were small (there being no scenes) and better order kept among the company that came; which made very good people think a play an innocent diversion for an idle hour or two, the plays being then, for the most part, more instructive than moral.

Historia Histrionica   1699

Before the Puritans' closure of the theatres in 1642 it would have been reasonable to describe the London theatre, in both senses of the adjective, as a popular art. In the first case it was popular simply by virtue of numbers—Harbage calculates that in Shakespeare's time 13% of the population of London went to the theatre every week, and three times that number went on public holidays[1]. 'In London', wrote Busino in 1618, 'theatrical representations without end prevail throughout the year in various parts of the city, and are invariably frequented by crowds of persons devoted to pleasure.' Later ages came to believe that anything which is immediately popular cannot be 'art', and came to mistrust work that gave immediate pleasure to large audiences, but the theatre of the Tudor and Stuart eras, with its crowds devoted to pleasure, and its most popular author the greatest writer in the English language, stands in permanent refutation of the belief that excellence is invariably incompatible with popularity.

In 1660, the Monarchy restored, theatres were allowed to open once more, but under firm restrictions. In the capital only two theatres were granted patents to present the legitimate drama, and those Londoners with a taste for the drama, who could afford the time, and the increased admission charges, now visited the small new playhouses at Drury Lane and at Lincoln's Inn Fields. However, describing what happened there as the *Restoration* of the theatre is a misnomer. In Shakespeare's theatre the play had been the thing. In the new theatre the socialising of the audience was as important as the play, and the diaries of Pepys and his contemporaries make it clear that the theatre had become an after-dinner diversion for the fashionable. It was a diversion in which the state bureaucrats had a close interest and when, following the act of 1737, the Lord Chamberlain became the official censor and licenser of plays, the power of the state officials to control the theatre was very great. An author could no longer simply write for himself or for his audience; now he had to write in a way acceptable to a widening spectrum of government censors, government licensers and government-appointed patent holders, whose actions took little account of the pleasures of ordinary folk, but who had a vested interest in placating the interests of the powerful and well-connected.

The struggle to 'free' the stage from the restrictions imposed by the support of the patent theatres, which culminated in the *1843 Theatres Act*, has been well documented[2]. Certainly the spirit behind that act was populist; a genuine feeling that both London and the drama would be better served if state control were lessened, and if plays were, like books, available in a free market. There was a sense in which that act was an opportunity for a genuine restoration of a kind of simpler, popular theatre that had produced the plays of Shakespeare, and why that opportunity was plainly missed is the theme of this book.

For there is no doubt that, in the hundred and forty years since the 'freeing' of our theatres, the opportunity *has* been missed. Our contemporary London theatre cannot be described, in either sense, as popular, and it seems likely that the capital may soon be left, on the larger scale at least, with only the National and Royal Shakespeare Companies. If that were to happen it would be ironic indeed. For it would mean that after the struggle to free the stage, the great designs and huge commercial ambitions of the West End managers, the campaigns and the self righteousness of the state bureaucrats, the decades of theorising and cant, and the fortunes made and lost, London will have been returned to where it stood in the eighteenth and early nineteenth century, its theatre dominated by two quasi-state organisations. And then, as an anonymous author wrote of the two competing London companies in 1702, 'After this, they traverse each other with uncertain fortune, this sometimes up, and that sometimes down, so that 'tis hard to say which is most like to prevail.' [3]

Attempts to explain this failure usually take one of two forms. The most popular explanation is that there exists an intangible and capricious commodity called public taste, which the theatrical profession, and the West End manager in particular, tries to comprehend and to meet. By such an account there will be times when ordinary folk choose to attend the drama, times when it is taken up by the privileged and fashionable, and times, sadly, such as our own, when the taste of all classes seems to be for other pleasures, and theatres stand forlorn and empty. The account that follows demonstrates that such an historical account is misleading. After 1865 the ordinary folk who had, for a short time, enjoyed the new populist theatre, did not *choose* to take their pleasures elsewhere; they were, by a series of deliberate managerial decisions, excluded from the new respectable theatre of the later Victorian age. The support of the favoured new audiences was sufficient to maintain the London theatre for a period until the managers' lack of response to the changing conditions of the first World War, and its aftermath, eroded that support too. Even the fashionable did not *choose* to depart; they were, in part, frozen out by a collective incompetence, an inflexibility in the face of competition from cinema, radio and television that would, in most other concerns, have been condemned as gross negligence.

The second explanation, sometimes intermingled with the first, is economic. By this account theatre managers have been caught since the middle of Victoria's reign by the spiralling costs of staging plays in the ways the public demanded. Then the managers have no option, given their selfless devotion to their art, but to woo the rich and favoured in order to fill their stalls and meet their costs. 'The present expense of a first class theatre', was what forced Squire Bancroft to throw out the pittites and replace them on the ground floor with the fashionable stalls at the Haymarket in 1880. And it was a pure devotion to 'the noble cause of the theatrical art' which led Henry Irving to increase his production costs more than tenfold during the twenty years of his Lyceum management. The theatre, it would seem, is caught in an economic trap not of its own making. Its costs must inevitably rise, faster than any general inflation, and it must *inevitably* turn to a shrinking audience for its income. There have even been attempts, which have found some favour amongst the arts bureaucrats, to claim that the performing arts are, by their very natures, caught in an economic dilemma from which only state aid, generously applied, can rescue them.[4]

This book points out that no such inevitability exists. We can produce plays in a hundred different styles, cheaply, expensively, simply or with great technical complexity, but audiences do not, as it were, indicate in advance what style they are to demand for each coming decade. It is the theatre professionals who choose, and who lead their own audiences in a manner and style which they have created. Theatrical style is not formed by any *vox populi*. When Bancroft spoke of 'the present expense of a first class theatre' he was speaking of a kind of theatre which he had largely chosen to create, not one which the population of London had demanded. That population had shown itself indeed to be as moved by Dickens' solo readings, for all their simplicity and cheap staging, as by the Bancrofts' detailed staging of their society dramas, with all their complexity and expense. Moreover Bancroft's assertion that he could not meet the expenses of his Haymarket productions unless he increased the number of ten shilling stalls is, as we shall presently see, a lie. It was no more *necessary* to get rid of the pit than, as we shall also see, Irving's spiralling production expenses were necessary.

Theatre, and most particularly West End theatre, has protected itself from scrutiny by insisting that theatre management is a mysterious practice which the ordinary man could not hope to understand. 'I think that Andree went up in his balloon', Pinero wrote ruefully to Archer in 1898, 'not to discover the North Pole, but to obtain an accurate survey of the Actor Manager' [5]. From the heyday of the West End, in the 1890s, to the early 1960s, West End managements in particular took a delight in the enclosed world they inhabited, and kept their financial records secret, their contractual arrangements private and their aims obscure. Unlike their Broadway equivalents, who blazoned their investments, running costs and income to the world, the British managers kept a club-like confidentiality.

Moreover they encouraged the layman to think that there was in the very *nature* of theatre, an inbuilt continuous cost escalation. We were always allowed to think that there were innumerable costs tied to arcane theatrical processes (of which the layman knew nothing) which inevitably put up the costs of production in the theatre far quicker than the costs of production of any other goods or service. Indeed, over the last thirty years, such a view has gained a measure of academic respectability, with economic writers claiming that the labour-intensive form of theatre means that, *inevitably*, its production costs must rise more quickly than those concerns which can cut labour costs and substitute the machine. Harold Baldry, for example, in his otherwise admirable book *A Case For The Arts* wishes to accept the truth of this. He quotes from a letter to *The Times* by Professor Walter Newlyn:

'The performing arts constitute the most extreme case of labour-intensive industry, and *Hamlet* requires as many man-hours to perform as when it was written. But since Shakespeare's day a science-based industrial revolution has made possible continuous reduction in the man-hours required for all material products. It follows that the performing arts must become relatively more costly over time unless the wages of performers are reduced or subsidies increased in real terms.' [6]

It is surprising, first, that in a book which is so well documented in other respects, Baldry allows the hidden assumptions in the paragraph to slide by, and indeed slide by with his implicit approval.

For *Hamlet* does *not* require 'as many' man-hours to perform as when it was written. It 'requires' many more. Shakespeare's company rehearsed and presented the play in a few days, with a company of highly experienced actors, but with little stage dressing and no lighting, and with few additional staff. When Henry Irving's company presented *Hamlet* on 30th December 1878, more than £4,000 had been spent during the fortnight's rehearsal, and each evening some 90 actors and supernumeraries, assisted by some 30 off-stage staff, were found necessary to present it. When one of our national companies now presents the play in London it will usually cost more than £150,000. There will be many more people involved off-stage than Irving found necessary, fewer people employed on-stage, and the rehearsal period (during which everyone will be paid) will be considerably longer. In other words the technical and business practices managers choose to adopt affect the total of man-hours involved to a very high degree. Labour costs have risen because our theatre managers have employed more (off-stage, rather than on) men for more paid hours, not because the 'same' man-hours cost more.

And the cost of the actors—who were virtually the only people involved in calculating the man-hours involved in presenting *Hamlet* when it was written—has through the years actually formed a diminishing part of the overall budget of London production. If we assume that in Shakespeare's day the wages of the actors represented some 80% of production and running costs, then it is clear that by Irving's time other costs had become much more important, for actors' wages during his Lyceum management (1879-1899) represented only 33% of total expenditure. And in the present West End it is rare for actors' wages to exceed 15% of total costs, so it would have little effect if we merely cut that expenditure. In the modern British theatre in part costs escalate through employing very many more people *off-stage*—not merely to run the stage machinery which, according to Newlyn's view, should have put many of them out of a job, but to join the ever-swelling army of PR experts, design consultants, publicity directors, technical advisers and marketing officers now considered a normal part of presenting a play. [7]

In part too the escalating costs of West End production have derived from a habit that we term 'conspicuous consumption' in a later chapter—a phrase which was first used by Thorstein Veblen in 1899 to describe a public means by which would-be superior persons raised themselves above mere trade. Thirdly the higher costs derive from the West End's notorious inability to refrain from bouts of internal commercial warfare, so that rents, rates and other related charges are often forced too high. Finally escalating costs are caused by the habit of hiring out to specialised interests each element in a production, so that it may well be designed, costumed, lit, wigged and promoted by five different firms, each anxious to charge profitable fees to the producers. In J. B. Priestley's words, 'Money is wasted, especially on sets, properties and costumes, because the management cannot undertake its own work and also because nearly everything has to be done at the last minute.' [8]

What then do production and running costs in the post-war West End look like? Joe Gatty gives a 'typical budget' for the contemporary West End theatre [9]:

Production Costs

	Musical	Play
Scenery and Properties	125,000	20,000
Costumes	50,000	8,000
Sound and Lighting	25,000	2,000
Salaries for actors, musicians and staff	75,000	12,000
Fees to Director, designers, choreographer, etc.	25,000	10,000
Theatre rent and charges	25,000	10,000
Fit up of set and lighting	15,000	5,000
Travel and set transport	5,000	1,500
Printing, advertising and publicity	60,000	20,000
Management Fees	4,000	2,000
Legal fees and insurance	5,000	1,000

Casting and audition expenses	5,000	1,000
Orchestration and music-copying	30,000	-
Rehearsal rooms, scripts, etc.	5,000	1,500
Sundries	6,000	1,000
	£460,000	**£95,000**

Running Costs (Weekly)

	Musical	Play
Salaries - actors and staff	12,000	3,250
- musicians	4,500	-
- theatre staff	6,000	2,500
- national insurance	2,000	600
- holiday provision	800	200
Theatre - rent	10,000	3,000
- light, heat and other charges	1,500	1,000
Publicity	2,000	1,500
Hire of equipment	2,500	500
Management Fee	500	400
Insurance	250	50
Royalties - authors	3,750	1,125
- director, choreographer	2,000	450
- management	500	150
Sundries (cleaning, replacements, etc.)	1,200	200
	£50,000	**£15,000**

Such costs have of course risen with inflation in recent years—*The Mousetrap* was first presented in 1952 for less than £3,000—but an examination of the categories will show that the cost of man-hours is a small proportion of the total, and that a number of the expenses exist because the managers have chosen to organise it like that. There is nothing in the nature of *Hamlet* that demands fees and royalties on such a scale *must* be paid to Director, Designer and 'Management' when it is now presented in the West End. It is managements who decide that a play written to be performed in contemporary dress and without scenery should now be expensively set and costumed when it is given in London.

Further, to continue with Professor Newlyn's assumptions, it is our theatre managements that have, for their own reasons, chosen not to acknowledge those changes which the 'science-based industrial revolution' *could* have made in theatre practice. It was, as we shall see later in the book, the West End theatre managers who chose non-co-operation with the cinema industry and with radio, and who have created only the most tenuous strands of co-operation with the television industry. For it is the case that the West End has, at times, quite deliberately recoiled from attracting a mass audience (through the media or by other means) to its product, preferring the kudos which exclusivity brings.

The managers have, in a word, chosen to arrange their affairs so that their costs have disproportionately risen over the years, and have so arranged things that with equal 'inevitability', they have had to rely on the high prices paid by the rich and fashionable or (in more recent times) have had to look for industrial or state sponsorship to balance their budgets. The implication is that matters are out of the managers' hands—that ordinarily they would certainly wish to serve a less privileged audience, but that the harsh economic realities forbid it. When they do sell a work to a television or film company so that it does reach a wider audience, it is an exception, and is not (we are told) something which should be regularly done.

So, in present circumstances, it will seem to the observer that our theatre must revert to its eighteenth century situation, with a dwindling audience of the privileged, and a few patrons, keeping the drama alive. But an examination, not of an economic model, but of the shaping points in the developments of the West End will show conclusively that it is like that because the collective actions of the managers have made it like that. The working classes deserted the London theatre because they were excluded by identifiable managerial decisions; that is, booking became extremely difficult for the ordinary person, the socialising, dressing up and the 'extras' associated with the refined West End theatre were beyond the means of ordinary folk, and (most important) theatres were built in the new West End which had virtually no place within them where the unprivileged were welcome.

In crude economic terms the unit costs of theatre management (which we might simply define as the costs of production per occupied seat) have also risen *because we have in each age built theatres smaller,* and have chosen first to shrink, then to exclude, popular areas such as the pit from our buildings. In 1840 the patent houses averaged 3,030 capacity. By the outbreak of the war in 1914, after two waves of theatre building, the average size of a West End theatre was a little over 1,000. By 1960 it was roughly 850. [*10*]

The thesis therefore is that by adopting a luxurious and extravagant style of management, and presenting plays with ever-growing armies of supporting 'experts' in ever-shrinking venues, it is the managers themselves who, collectively, have created 'the crisis of the West End'. The charge against them is not that they have been commercial, but in one important sense, that they have not *been commercial enough*. And if the charge were *merely* one of inept management, it would perhaps be only a matter of amusement to theatre historians, for we may well say that it was merely a local aberration. But their century and more of mismanagement is much more serious than that. For together with the lush style of management that they created for themselves, the West End managers sought, and defended, a position of total control over the theatre throughout the country. Between 1865 and 1914 (and afterwards, to a lessened degree) West End theatre *was* British theatre; their distortion of the nature of theatre became the national distortion; their mismanagement became our general mismanagement of theatre, and their snobbery became a pervasive national snobbery over what had been once a popular art.

For in saying that snobbery was the besetting sin of West End management we are saying that their actions were motivated not by any simple commercial ambition, but by a desire to join a particular rank of society. Theirs was not a simple class ambition. They did not act to make a profit from a working class, nor to create fortunes (although this they occasionally achieved almost by inadvertancy). They acted always so that theatre folk could join that supreme *rank* that great painters already enjoyed, that of *artists*, and could mix with Royalty, intellectuals and heroes as equals. Their snobbery was of a classic kind; they sought the favours of the cultured, not the favours of the rich. It was an ambition that was realised by the end of the nineteenth century, when the leaders of the West End were able with Irving to join that society that they so much enjoyed, and in which Noel Coward and his friends later luxuriated, the British Cultural Establishment.

And as membership of the highest rank of society is defined in its simplest form by the company you keep, we should not be surprised to find that, from the moment Marie Bancroft exulted in the line of carriages outside the Prince of Wales's theatre in 1865, the West End has been primarily concerned, whether it is 'efficient' business or not, to keep company with the fashionable and rich, and to ignore the majority. It is for example noticeable, when looking at West End business in the latter years of the nineteenth century, that events which have a profound effect upon working class lives and incomes do not disturb West End audiences. The great dockers' strike of 1889 for example, did not affect that theatre at all. However in the following year, when the City bankers Baring's collapsed, theatres emptied and booking fell to nothing [11]. And there is every evidence that the West End continued to maintain its posture throughout our period. In 1956, when impresario Henry Sherek was worried about the possible effects on the Criterion audiences of a total bus strike, he was reassured by veteran actor Wilfrid Hyde White. 'My dear fellow, you cannot make me believe that our clientele come to the Criterion theatre in buses.' He was perfectly right. The theatre did not have an empty seat throughout the strike. [12]

The managers themselves would of course, certainly before 1960, not have made any attempt to refute the charge of snobbery. Their explanation would have been that their overspending and small luxury theatres were a part of a style that they had chosen and that, within its confines, it worked perfectly well. Some would have agreed to the charge even more cheerfully. Peter Daubeny, for example, wrote in 1952:

> 'Snobbery is at best of course a romantic impulse. It is the enjoyment of boredom in distinguished company. As such, it is almost a Christian virtue, eminently defensible.' [13]

'The enjoyment of boredom in distinguished company' is a perfect description of the essential West End experience. There is about it nothing of the populist, or the raw and exciting theatre of Shakespeare; more than anything, it is like the weary rituals of which Pepys often wrote:

> 'The house infinite full, and the prologue most silly, and the play, though admirable, yet had no pleasure almost in it, because just the very same design, and words, and sense, and plot, as every one of his plays have, any one of which alone would be admirable, whereas so many of the same design and fancy do but dull one another; and this, I perceive, is the sense of everybody else as well as myself.' [14]

In any examination of prime West End theatre, an audience sitting through drama of the 'very same design', but nevertheless plainly, like Pepys, enjoying their boredom, will seem common enough. It is an experience which has within it an appearance of discrimination, but is in fact highly ritualised; for a certain rank flattering and narcissistic, reassuring them by its very predictability that company and social setting are suitably distinguished, but for others it is meaningless and dull. The harm that the West End wrought was both to establish such a huge mass of outsiders who became strangers to the theatre, while insisting that the West End rituals, virtually impenetrable to that mass, were the summit of the national drama.

Yet, briefly, in the 1840s, there were signs that the theatre was to develop as the instigators of the 1843 Act had hoped, and was to become a popular art once more. It is with that decade that our description begins.

The Adelphi in the 1840s. London theatres drew their audiences with few, if any modern publicity techniques. There was no advance booking, and the theatres did not have 'fronts' in the manner that became common by the end of the century.

2
Popular London Theatre, 1840 and after

Robertson told me that Sir H. Wheatley had, on the part of the Queen, expressed a wish that the price of her box should be reduced from £400 to £350. If this be Royal Patronage, commend me to popular favour!

William Charles Macready.   Diary, September 24, 1837

It was in the Nineteenth Century that West End theatre was created. After the passing of the *1843 Theatres Act*, when the monopoly of the patent houses was broken, all theatres were once more placed upon an equal footing. In a century of vast British expansion, during which the population of the United Kingdom rose from 16,345,646 to 40,921,371 and its trade rose from £67,300,000 to £814,570,000, it might have seemed that the drama, in all its forms, would become generally available throughout the kingdom. The new industrial towns and cities contained vast new potential audiences—with the enforced leisure time that the industrial shift system gave, some spare money for recreation and, increasingly, the rudiments of education. It seemed likely, to some people at least, that after 1843 theatres would be built in large numbers and that a range of dramatic entertainments—some developing particular forms appropriate to particular areas—would proliferate in Britain. In London most of all it seemed to be an appropriate time for theatres to be built and run throughout the city; some serving the thickly-populated areas that were newly built on both sides of the river, and other, specialist, houses that would serve the whole population but which could be located anywhere within its boundaries.

At the beginning of the century, when the state of the drama was talked of, the restrictive law meant that in effect it was the state of the patent houses that was discussed. In the second half of the century

21

however, talk of the state of the drama *might* have ranged over the work of particular companies in Sheffield, Nottingham or Birmingham, in addition to the condition of the various companies in London. When the state of *music* was debated it was the festivals, choirs and orchestras throughout the country that were scrutinised, and it seemed that it was as likely that 'the drama' might have encompassed the special centres of excellence in Attercliffe, Bulwell or Selly Oak, but it did not. Towards the end of the century what was usually available in each town and city was a rough copy of the style of proscenium arch performance, managerial practices and social rituals that were generated by the theatre known as 'West End'. A new London theatrical establishment, aiming to please the most fashionable Victorian society, preferring always a highly ritualised theatre catering directly for the privileged to any of the rougher and more generally accessible forms that had often characterised British drama in earlier centuries, had established a near-monopoly of theatre practice so narrow in its social ambitions, and yet so powerful in its creation of new managerial and artistic conventions to realise them, that the administration of contemporary British theatre still lives under its shadow.

West End theatre came to be located within that fashionable rectangle bounded by the Strand, Kingsway, Oxford Street and New Bond Street. However by no means all of the theatres located within it were necessarily considered to be West End, while some of those set outside it sometimes were, for the term West End referred as often to an amalgam of fashionable London conventions as to a particular locality. Thus the Prince of Wales's theatre in the 1870s was essentially West End, although it was situated off Tottenham Court Road and outside the fashionable area, whereas the first music halls that were built within the charmed mile were most decidedly not.

Therefore West End theatre must not be thought of simply as central London theatre. It did not establish itself where it did because that particular part of the middle of London was a convenient central point for most people who lived in the capital. The area around Piccadilly was for instance a considerable distance from the new railway stations, and the underground did not open stations in Piccadilly and Leicester Square until 1906. Those 'provincial people' who came 'up to town every night' and who according to Hollingshead's testimony to the *1866 Select Committee on Theatrical Licences and Regulations* formed a considerable part of the theatre audience, must in many cases have had a very long walk or an expensive cab ride to and from their destinations.

22

It was inconvenient in other ways; there was little parking space for private carriages, and central London jams were frequent. An 1848 description from the *Illustrated London News* sounds disturbingly familiar:

'Some heavily-laden waggon has broken down, and the long line of carriages of every description are suddenly brought to a stand-still—all are motionless. You see the old thoroughbred London cabman, who has promised to take his fare either east or west, as the matter may be, in a given number of minutes,—dodge in and out for a few seconds . . . until he comes to the entrance of some narrow street, the ins and outs of which are known only to a few like himself when, crack, bang, and he has vanished, giving one of his own peculiar leers at parting, at the long line he has left stationary.' [1]

Nor were the reasons for the siting of the theatres in that area ordinary commercial ones; land and labour were very much more costly than in other areas of the city in which, for example, the administrators of the professional sports clubs chose to site their grounds.

It was not however becase it made straightforward commercial sense, or because they wished to give a good service to the public at large that led the theatrical establishment, in the 1860s and after, to build and trade in that part of the city. It was because that area was in three important ways becoming the fashionable heart of London. First, it was the centre of London's growing clubland. As Walter Besant remarked in 1909, 'The development of the West End club has been a very remarkable sign of the times during the last fifty years', marking 'an ever-increasing desire for separation and exclusion'[2]. Second it was the fashionable centre for shopping; the exclusive emporia of Bond Street and Regent Street creating, as the *Architect* said in 1873, 'a field of special West End businesses'[3]. Third, although the days of Mayfair and St. James's as residential districts drew to a close in the 1890s, it was the centre for the exclusive social engagement; at venues such as Almacks, in St. James, were held the assembly balls, receptions and other social events of London's season. Overall, the West End was where the fashionable, for eighty years, found it *de rigeur* to go and to be seen. Irene Vanbrugh describes the Sunday dress and habits of that society that the later Victorian theatre stars joined:

'Everybody who was anybody knew they would meet their friends there as they all slowly paraded up and down in their smart Sunday clothes, the men as meticulously dressed as the women. Anything but a frock coat and top hat would have been unheard of. This rigid rule about men's clothes was carried to an incredible severity and no young society man would have dared to walk down Piccadilly even on a week day except in the orthodox costume.' [4]

If you wished to join that fashionable society, and to gain its approval, then it was essential to be established upon its territory. It was neither a cheap nor, as regards the majority of Londoners, a convenient nor a congenial neighbourhood, but, if you aspired above almost everything to join the higher ranks of society, it was an essential one.

In the 1840s however, no such concentration had occurred. The two patent houses, the central theatres and suburban houses took their place in a plethora of entertainment that was scattered through the city. The emphasis was on the spectacular and the large-scale in both audience provision and presentation. The patent houses themselves were huge; In 1843 Drury Lane accommodated 3,060, and Covent Garden 3,000. Other theatres were almost as large. The central King's theatre held 2,500, and elsewhere the East London theatre in Stepney held 2,150, the Standard in Shoreditch 3,400 and the Surrey in Lambeth 2,800. Throughout the forties and fifties the tendency was always to rebuild on the largest possible scale. The Brittania in Hoxton was rebuilt in 1858 to hold 5,000, and the hall built on the site of the former Surrey Zoological Gardens held more than 10,000 seated spectators and had space for 1,000 musicians.

Crowds for all types of entertainment were vast. Astley's, which presented a kind of horse-riding drama, held 3,780. The Pleasure Gardens accommodated large crowds; even so small a pleasure garden as that laid out on the ground to the east of the Eagle tavern in City Road attracted between 5,000 and 6,000 a night. A larger gardens, such as the Vauxhall (which re-opened in 1841) or the Cremorne gardens, set between the Thames and King's Road, Chelsea, could easily take five times that number; at the Cremorne the dance floor alone was large enough for 4,000 dancers and a band of 50. Equally large crowds attended the Regent's Park Zoo, and promenaded in the parks or studied natural wonders at Kew Gardens. Scattered through the city were peep shows and curiosities, ranging from a new and elegant diorama housed by Regent's Park, to the freakshow booths at Greenwich, and Gilbert B. Cross calculates in *Next Week—East Lynne* that the simplest London halls, the penny 'blood tubs' in which

24

Huge crowds gathered for all manner of public entertainments,
whether it was the charity schools singing at Crystal Palace (top)
or Mr. M'Collum's Equestrian act at Drury Lane (bottom)

The Victorians became adept at building large grandstands, as well
as large auditoriums. Here are the stands at Ascot (top) and a
temporary stand at Vauxhall Gardens, erected for the crowd
watching the balloon ascent of Mr. Green in his 'Victoria Balloon'
(bottom). Note the illumination by electric spotlight.

primitive melodrama was played, must have attracted a total of more than 50,000 during the pantomime season. [5]

There was a noticeable upsurge in the presentation of outdoor spectacle; firework displays, open air concerts and bank holiday carnival stunts attracted huge crowds to the gardens. Sporting events in the forties did particularly well. Crowds of over 20,000 to important cricket matches were common, and even in 1843, when the summer was wet, 'the teeming multitude' flocked to Ascot Heath for the Derby. Large gatherings were attracted to unlikely locations for such brutal diversions as cock fighting (banned in 1859), prize fighting and (until this too was prohibited in 1868) public executions. 10,000 gathered in Bodmin to see an execution in 1840, and, more gruesome still, a special train ran from London in 1849 to Norwich to take sightseers to swell the crowd at the public execution of Rush.

It is all too easy to draw simple conclusions about the popular taste from even so brief a survey of the kinds of pastime which were available in London in the 1840s. The popularity of the spectacles, of the gaudy and the gruesome, does not necessarily tell us everything about the limits of the Victorian imagination, or the boundaries of the popular taste. Great crowds did not gather for their entertainment throughout the city as a result of some kind of general act of discrimination, but often for more mundane reasons.

First was the fact that for many of London's new inhabitants it was, by the 1840s, better to be almost anywhere than inside your own home. London's population had risen from 959,000 in 1800 to nearly 3,000,000, of whom, according to the 1851 census, more than three quarters could be classified as working class. The living conditions for most were dreadful. As G. M. Trevelyan says in *English Social History:*

> 'Still throughout the forties nothing was done to control the slum-landlords and jerry-builders who, according to the prevalent *laissez faire* philosophy, were engaged from motives of self-interest in forwarding the general happiness. These pioneers of "progress" saved space by crowding families into single rooms or thrusting them underground into cellars, and saved money by the use of cheap and insufficient building material, and by providing no drains—or, worse still, by providing drains that oozed into the water supply. In London, Lord Shaftesbury discovered a room with a family in each of its four corners, and a room with a cesspool immediately below its boarded floor.' [6]

In the 1842 report *Sanitary Conditions of the Labouring Classes* Chadwick, Kay and others reported on the 'unmitigated slum' that stretched from the river through Stepney and Poplar to Bethnal Green, Shoreditch and Finsbury, affecting Bermondsey and Southwark on the south bank. More than a million Londoners were living in domestic conditions of such insanitary poverty that to analyse their attendance at a cheap carnival, or a simple street entertainment or even a public execution in terms of the popular *taste* seems to be wrong.

Second, commenting upon the popularity of the spectacular we must not miss the spiritual importance of colour. The housing and industrial plant of working class London were not only insanitary and dangerous, but dark, sooty and drab. Dickens' depressing descriptions of the less salubrious parts of the city in *Oliver Twist* (1838) and *Nicholas Nickleby* (1839) are well known. Less well known is the reaction of Herman Melville who arrived in London in November 1849 and found it, wreathed in clouds of smoke, a 'city of Dante'. In the same month the *Illustrated London News* remarked that even St. Paul's was 'blackened and encrusted with a hard mixture of cement and smoke, cobwebs and rain' [7]. The poor wore the drabbest of colours, made blacker by the polluted air. They worked in dark, ill-ventilated rooms, and the lighting in their lodgings was equally bad. When mass pleasures offered—as did the peepshows, the pleasure gardens and the theatres in their three different ways—an antidote of vivid colour, the polarity has a near-moral significance. This was most strongly suggested in Dickens' parabolical novel *Hard Times* (1854) in which the vivid colour of the visiting circus represents a life-enhancing force within the ashen utilitarianism of industrial Coketown.

In large-scale popular amusements there was an insistent emphasis upon arresting colour; 'colourful' was one of the most frequently used words in early Victorian advertising, and there was as much interest in the colouring of concert halls, decorative garden houses, assembly rooms and theatres as there was in the design and colour of the entertainment itself. Before the opening of the Great Exhibition of 1851 for example there was considerable public debate over the internal decoration of the Crystal Palace:

> 'The contest respecting the decoration of the interior is by no means quieted: the advocates for employing a bronze colour are warmer than ever, relying for their strong point upon the metallic character of the material; all confidence in the strength of the

columns, says they, is lost, if you paint them in colours used for wooden poles. Employ iron grey, with a relief of gold, exclaims another party. We ourselves heard a third counsellor suggest a *bamboo cane* hue, to preserve the lightness of the structure.' [8]

The Great Exhibition itself may be seen as the peak of the instinct towards the spectacular and the large scale. On shilling days it accommodated 70,000 people, and during the 140 days of the exhibition Messrs Schweppe, manufacturers of soda water, who had paid £5,500 for the catering rights, sold 934,691 Bath buns, 870,027 plain buns and 1,092,337 bottles of mineral water. Strong drink was not permitted. Nor was cooking permitted within the building, so food was cold. The banning of cooking by the caterers was part of a desire to make the Great Exhibition sweeter smelling than other London places of amusement were.

In the most general terms it is easy therefore to show that Londoners had, in the twenty years following the 1843 act, a variety of popular diversions, and that in the 1840s at least the theatres took their place successfully among them. And, to an extent, there was a common managerial philosophy; the theatres, entertainment houses such as the Egyptian Hall in Piccadilly, the various pleasure gardens, and the song and supper rooms had much in common in their programming. The emphasis was on a variety, in which the freed drama took its place with dioramas, music, ballet, fireworks and horse-riding. As a visitor to the Eagle exclaimed in 1841:

> 'Song, dance, opera, farce and ballet all relieve each other, and the visitor is sure to go away delighted with the entertainment the worthy caterer has provided for him.' [9]

Common too was a belief in low pricing. The prevailing ethic was that it was always better to attract a large crowd paying low admission, together with a belief in the Londoner's right to mix drinking with the enjoyment of entertainment. The Eagle visitor of 1841 went on, 'But, as if this were not enough, other enchantments await him. Brandy and ballet dancing, grog and glees, cakes and catches, with cigars and cascades, all allure the palate, enchant the eye and delight the ear'. The manager of the Eagle, Thomas Rouse, in fact offset his theatrical losses by his profits in the tavern—a technique we believe, wrongly, to belong to modern arts administration.

In the most general terms, it can also be said that many managers of entertainment found their work, in the 1840s, relatively safe and profitable. Entertainments as diverse as the tour of 'General' Tom Thumb by Barnum in 1844, the 'magical entertainment' at the Egyptian Hall and the appearance of Jenny Lind at Her Majesty's theatre in 1847, when the demand to get in was so great that 'Ladies were carried off their feet and they and their escorts were shoved against columns and walls', all attracted huge audiences through publicity methods which we should regard as casual and low-key. Many of the theatres (with the exception of the patent houses, which succeeded only intermittently) were in regular, though rarely in excessive, profit. Webster made a 'very considerable profit' on the 1840/41 season at the Haymarket, but a more modest one during the remainder of the forties. Keeley broke even during his three years 1844-47 Lyceum management, eventually resigning in part because of the grumbling of Strutt, his financial backer, who resented the annual £2,500 rental he was asked to pay to the theatre owners. Lumley's seasons at Her Majesty's theatre were profitable in 1843, 1844 and 1845, and very profitable in 1847 and 1848, when grand opera and the more homely fare at the Brittania, Standard and the Surrey attracted equally large audiences. Public response was (inevitably, as there was virtually no advance booking system) immediate and strong to a favoured piece, and after five days a new play could be a 'hit'. Boucicault gave something of the excitement of such immediate success when he wrote to his mother after the opening of *London Assurance* in 1841:

'On Thursday last March 4, a comedy in 5 Acts written by me was played at Covent Garden theatre, and has made an unparalleled hit, indeed so much so that it is played *every night* to crammed houses and is expected to run the whole season'. [10]

However such success was more usually achieved through regular changes of both titles and genres. As Figure 1 shows, only 4 London dramas had runs of more than 100 performances in the 1840s, against 16 in the 1850s and 52 in the 1860s. They were *The Chinese War* (Astley's, 1844; 114 performances), *How To Settle Accounts With Your Laundress* (Adelphi, 1847; 108 p.), *The Island of Jewels* (Lyceum, 1849; 111 p.), and *Martin Chuzzlewit* (Lyceum, 1844; 105 p.).

The script is extant of Planche's burlesque *The Island of Jewels*. From internal evidence we can say something about the nature of a big London audience (its attendance was probably in total close to 200,000, as it opened on Boxing Day and was London's most successful show of a generally successful Christmas season). The sequence of

	Figure 1		
	Long runs in London's Theatres 1840-1940		
	Over 100 perfs	**Over 200 perfs**	**Over 300 perfs**
1840s	4	0	0
1850s	16	0	0
1860s	52	11	6
1870s	107	25	9
1880s	157	46	22
1890s	169	58	25
1900s	192	73	39
1910s	308	138	70
1920s	406	191	93
1930s	353	143	66

scenes for example shows the love of spectacle and colour; a court-room, a lonely seashore, a jewel-encrusted palace, a basaltic cavern, a rocky mountain pass, followed by a spectacular transformation to the colonnade upon which the jewels of the title were rediscovered. It is moreover written with rather more wit and point than is credited by some critics of the genre; references to the 'Railway King' (pp. 16/17—all page references are to Lacy's Acting Edition of 1850), the card sharp (p.19) and the dealings of the City (p.22) require up-to-date knowledge of contemporary events. That a higher degree of literacy is sometimes expected may be gauged from the references to *King Lear* (p.32), *Othello* (p.22) the pastiches of *Macbeth* (p.16) and *Romeo and Juliet* (p.24), and that some of the popular audience was expected to be *au fait* with other arts movements is indicated by references to other artists, such as the joke about Titian (p.20). There were incidental ballets, and spectacular costume and that the piece combined popular with critical approval is obvious from the enthusiastic notice in the *Illustrated London News* which said, 'Of all Mr. Planche's burlesques the present is perhaps the most elegant ever witnessed, and the way it has been produced the most gorgeous imaginable'. The writer continued, 'The concluding scene—the discovery in the midst of an unfolded colonnade of palm trees, seven nymphs supporting the crown jewels on a cushion—is indescribably magnificent. The whole, also, was in perfect taste; and the piece must be pronounced a crowning triumph in the art of burlesque.'

Such a critical reaction would not have been possible in the 1850s, during which it became hard, if not impossible, to credit a broadly popular entertainment with being an 'art' which was 'in perfect taste'. A minority audience, assumed to be discriminating and superior, was slowly detached from the mass. It was that audience which was to be seen as London's salon, the natural audiences for the arts, while the commoners were to be gratified at mere entertainments. The Great Exhibition played a notable part in shaping that division; first, in the way that through its own sharply varied admission prices it divided up the mass audience. Although the 500,000 crowd which assembled in Hyde Park for its opening was drawn from all classes, thereafter the total of 6,500,000 attenders was daily divided by their ability either to pay 5/- 'on the day of the great folks', or 1/- 'on the day of the little folks'. The differences were sharp:

> 'On one day, society—on the other, the world. On the one day, the Nave crowded in such fashion as opera corridors and Belgravian saloons are crowded, and the aisles and galleries empty. On the other day, the aisles and galleries crowded, and the Nave a thoroughfare—a street—swarming, bustling, pushing with loud voices and brusque movements; and people who have sharp elbows, and can use them, and who push along as in Fleet Street, or in Cheapside, intent upon going somewhere, determination in their muscles, and purpose in their eyes—the energetic business-like march of this energetic business-like nation.' [11]

The division was important because the Great Exhibition had a significant secondary effect; it emptied the city's other popular venues. The *Illustrated London News* of 17th March 1851, commented:

> 'But the Great Exhibition has its unpopular as well as its popular side. City merchants and their correspondents say that it has 'killed business' for the season, and they grumble accordingly. The caterers for the public amusements are still louder in their complaints. The theatres do not fill; panoramas are losing speculations; and people are so busy with the one Great Exhibition, that they cannot encourage any minor ones, or find time for them if they would.' [12]

Some theatres of course continued to thrive. Phelps' company at Sadler's Wells did well, and Charles Kean's first season at the Princess's Theatre was successful. It was the minor theatres, the penny gaffs and the old patent houses which notably suffered. The effect of the

An artist's impression of the great difference between the five shilling days (above) and the crowded one shilling days (below) at the Great Exhibition. Note that the artist views 'The Commoners' Day' from outside the Exhibition site.

Great Exhibition was in hastening the divide between the popular and the artistic, so that when Matthews and Vestris' management failed at the Lyceum in 1855 the *Illustrated London News* reflected the new view that their collapse was not because they had lost the large popular following of earlier years, but was caused by their neglect of 'the serious drama'. Success must now lie in the cultivation of a new London theatrical *Salon*. It was a refrain which was to be heard with increasing frequency in the following decade.

3
The Suburban Theatre and Samuel Phelps

The more poetical of Shakespeare's dramas have here been the most popular. The example thus successfully set is about to be followed elsewhere; and there is good reason to believe that the liberty now conceded to the stage has given a new start to the drama.

Athenaeum   August 1847

There have in our period been several examples of a good suburban theatre establishing a reputation greater than that of most of the central 'West End' venues, and drawing central London audiences. At roughly the same time as Henry Irving's Lyceum management, Sara Lane established a popular and well-run company at the Brittania, Hoxton. As remarkable was Lilian Baylis' eccentric but successful management of the Old Vic from 1898 to 1937, during which time it had its period as London's leading classical theatre, even though it was 'on the wrong side of the water'. More recently the gutsy partnership of Joan Littlewood and Gerry Raffles drew the theatrical elite, in the 1950s, to the Theatre Royal, Stratford East. It was however in the years immediately following the 1843 act that the most remarkable of these managements occurred.

In the 1840s and 1850s there were several notable Shakespeare seasons, and some managements enjoyed considerable success from revivals of his work. Certainly some of the productions of Shakespeare by Matthews and Vestris at the Lyceum between 1847 and 1856 were more successful than the general run of their productions, and in the 1850s London had not only the great success of Kean's Shakespearean seasons at the Princess's from 1850 to 1859, but the Brittania seasons of Shakespeare and William Creswick's Surrey productions. There was, amongst the vast audience for the big and spectacular, a large and serious audience for Shakespeare. Of all managements however the most remarkable is that of the actor Samuel Phelps, who left Macready's company at Drury Lane and (with another former member of Macready's company, Mrs Warner) took the lesseeship of Sadler's Wells theatre in 1844, remaining there as manager for 18 years, and presenting there all but four of Shakespeare's plays, and a considerable classical and contemporary repertoire.

Phelps' managerial achievement is not that he civilised an Islington wilderness, but that he drew the fashionable to the suburbs. In any case Sadler's Wells theatre was *not* a theatrical wilderness. In the previous year, 1843, productions had included *Faust, Venice Preserved,* Colman's *The Jealous Wife, Don Juan,* a sumptuous *A Christmas Carol, King Arthur, School for Scandal* and *The Merchant of Venice.* There had been from that area considerable agitation for the removal of the monopoly of the patent theatres. Far from being a depressed suburb Islington was a prosperous setting for the theatre. The combined population of Islington and Finsbury, which totalled 168,676 in the 1841 census, contained a considerable middle class. Looking back on the earlier years of Victorian London, the Rector of St. John's, the Reverend William Dawson wrote:

> 'Within the time covered by Her Majesty's happy reign, merchants, lawyers, doctors, wealthy watchmakers and jewellers lived in Red Lion Square and St. John's Square, and kept their carriages in adjacent mews.'[1]

After a year Phelps was to poke fun at the story that he had 'tamed' an uncivilised suburb. In September 1845 a solemn letter (signed by Phelps and his partner Mrs Warner, although whether they actually wrote it is unclear) appeared in the pages of *Punch*, detailing in mock-heroic style their 'missionary work':

> 'That on our taking Sadler's Wells . . . the natives of the immediate neighbourhood and surrounding villages were in a lamentable state of darkness as to the existence and humanising purposes of William Shakespeare'.[2]

It continues in the same tone, detailing the achievements of the new regime, among them that the natives no longer call for Grimaldi's popular songs, and that their morals are much improved[!]:

> 'Further, the night charges at the various police-stations of the neighbourhood have sensibly diminished; and men—before considered irredeemable bacchanals—are now nightly known to bring their wives and little ones to listen to the solemn and sportive

truths of Shakespeare, in the pit and gallery.' [3]

The authorship of this *Puff Oblique* is incertain, but the authorship of one of the scenes in the 1845 Christmas pantomime is quite definite:

> 'A first class carriage will be seen to contain Mrs Warner and Mr Phelps, leaving Drury Lane with a huge volume of Shakespeare; they soon alight at Sadler's Wells amidst the congratulations of the Islingtonians.' [4]

That scene contains within the caricature a more plausible picture. The people of Islington had agitated for their own legitimate theatre, and upon his arrival in Islington Phelps certainly received the congratulations and support of a significant part of the local population. 2,800 of them, for example, had come to his first night in 1844, already 'converted'.

There were of course a number of factors which influenced Phelps in his decision to assume the management of Sadler's Wells. First was his desire to have control of his own artistic destiny, and to play those parts which, while he was in Macready's company, he would not be given. Second was the fact that Sadler's Wells was a large theatre surrounded by a good potential audience for the serious drama, and third was the important fact that compared with the theatres in central London the rental was very low. At the Adelphi Webster paid an annual rental of £4,000, Drury Lane was £5,000 and in the 1850s Kean paid £4,000 a year for the Princess's. Sadler's Wells cost Phelps only £1,000 in rental, payable in 10 monthly instalments of £100 each.

When he began his management, his advertising offers two clear indications as to his immediate state. First, he plainly had to bring his company before the public very quickly, so that he had receipts with which to pay salaries, outstanding production costs and the first month's rental. Second, it seems likely that he trusted that the Islington audience would be large enough to spare him the expense of having to advertise in other than the immediate neighbourhood and in the local papers. His major expense was a handbill distributed to local householders to advertise *Macbeth*, his opening production. He supplemented this with a poster campaign in the immediate neighbourhood but, significantly, did not advertise in any other than the Islington papers; no announcement of the opening appeared in *The Times*. [5]

The circulated bill is interesting. After noting that the 1843 act has put 'all theatres upon an equal footing of security and respectability', it goes on to argue that theatres need not therefore be all in the centre of

London but could be set within each district:

> 'These circumstances justify the notion that each separate divison of an immense metropolis, with its 2,000,000 of inhabitants, may have its own well-conducted theatre within a reasonable distance of the homes of its patrons.'

They admitted that they commenced 'under the disadvantage of very short preparation' but trusted to 'the kind encouragement of the more highly educated and influential classes' of the neighbourhood, to help make 'Sadler's Wells theatre the resort of the respectable inhabitants of the neighbourhood, for the highest purpose of theatrical entertainment'. After which flattery Phelps added a simple 'introductory offer':

> 'Any patron with whom this circular is left, will on sending an address card to the box office, have an admission for One forwarded, as it is the wish of the management, and their motive for this departure from their otherwise strict system of giving no Orders, to afford to those who may take an interest in their plan, an opportunity of judging for themselves, and to speak of the undertaking as they may think it deserves.' [6]

The appeal was not only implicitly to those persons of standing in the area who already possessed an acquaintance with Shakespeare, but explicitly the means of gaining admission was by sending an address card—a clear means of filtering the unlettered from the audience. It is obvious that Phelps expected a substantial local middle class audience, but not one to which he would have to play tutor and missionary.

There is another piece of evidence that the audience for the classical productions was a middle class one. The evening's programme began at six thirty, which was too early for the poorer classes, whose working day, even after the *1847 Ten Hours Act*, rarely ended before seven o'clock. It was customary to let people in for half-price after nine o'clock so that if they chose they could see the climax of the major piece, and the 'after-piece' which was usually, although by no means always, something broad and popular. Phelps followed this custom. His early productions ran for a week, sometimes three days, but the after-pieces stayed in the programme through several major productions. It is likely then that he had a working class audience that visited the Wells less frequently than once a week and who were not able to interest themselves in the main attraction. They were therefore unaffected by the fact that it was changing regularly to suit the more leisured audience. Thus one after-

38

piece, Greenwood's *A Row in the Buildings* (already a local favourite), ran through the opening production *Macbeth*, then *Othello*, which followed it, and then through *The Provoked Wife* which followed that.

The runs of the major pieces were however too short for financial comfort. A week was not long enough to prepare a new production, and the income from so short a period was not high enough to meet the rental, regular salaries and such frequently-recurring production costs. The admission prices at the theatre were low, and like the other London managers, Phelps felt they must remain so:

Dress Circle	3s.
Second Circle	2s.
Gallery	6d.
Pit	1s.
Boxes	£1.11s.6d.

Although it is not possible to calculate with precision what the receipt was from a full house, we know that the pit held some 1,200, and although the admission system was so little under control that appeals had sometimes to be made from the stage before the show could commence asking some of the audience to go home, it would seem reasonable to assume that the £120 a maximum pit attendance gave was little less than a half of the total receipt, which was probably some £220-250. Therefore income from the pit was extremely important; Phelps did not, for example, permit children to enter it free, as the custom was elsewhere.

However, as the programme was changed so frequently, we may assume that the houses for the classic presentations, although good, were not maximum, and could at first sustain runs of only a few days (although it was sometimes possible to bring plays back into the repertoire). These were the classical productions of Phelps' first season, together with the total number of performances each achieved during the year:

Macbeth	14
Othello	10
The Provoked Wife	8
The Rivals	9
City Madam	13
The Bridal	30
Richard the Third	24
Hamlet	28

King John	21
School for Scandal	7
A New Way to Pay Old Debts	3
Merchant of Venice	6
Henry the Eighth	1
Road to Ruin	4
Wild Oats	3
The Jealous Wife	2
The Wonder	2

There were in addition some nine contemporary five-act dramas produced during the first season, with an average run of 8 performances each. The classical productions above had average runs of 11 performances. Over the whole season Phelps had to meet new production and advertising costs on average at every tenth performance.

He therefore, quite plainly, decided that he must widen his catchment area for his audience. He started a campaign in late summer to draw the central Londoners out to Islington. Mr Greenwood was replaced in the box office by Mr Notter 'late of Drury Lane and Covent Garden'. The varieties of posters printed, by Fairbrother and Son of Covent Garden, were increased, and two new outlets for ticket sales were added, one in New Bond Street.

From the increasing press attention that Sadler's Wells received after those first months, we might infer that Phelps started to attract numbers of what had been thought to be 'the' London audience out to join his Islington regulars. In 1847 *The Times* described his audience as comprising 'a singular number of literary men—and ladies—of the present day'. By the late forties reports were identifying notables, Dickens in particular, in the Sadler's Wells audience with remarkable frequency. By 1853 the outlets for ticket sales had increased to seven—including sites in Bond Street, New Bond Street, the Royal Library and Regent Street. Sadler's Wells by then was plainly a London theatre and not an Islington one.

There were two additional reasons why this should have been so. First, transport within the city was steadily improving. Although the two railway stations (Shoreditch Street and Fenchurch Street) which served the theatre were some little distance from it, each was connected to sections of central London and the East End, and each ran late night services. The journey was even simpler for travellers by Omnibus. First, Omnibuses increased greatly in number. When Phelps assumed his management there were some 800 in regular service; by 1850 there were more than 1,500. Although no omnibus route went directly past the theatre door—*The Times* suggested in February 1846 that intending visitors to the theatre should 'put all their faith in the Angel at Islington, and when there to trust to the nearest policeman or barber's shop for further particulars' [7] —stops in St. John Street, Clerkenwell Road, City Street and Clerkenwell Green were sufficiently close. More important still, their prices gradually decreased; increased competition, and the increase in capacity brought about by the introduction of knifeboard roof seats, meant that few if any of Phelps' distant audience would by the mid-1850s have had to pay more than 2d. to arrive at his theatre. Travel was therefore a decreasing deterrent to the distant audience.

Second, during Phelps' tenure of the Wells, Islington's own middle classes began to move out, and buy homes further North in Highgate and St. John's Wood. Partly this was caused by the opening of King's Cross Station in 1852, which brought a massive influx to the area. Islington's population trebled between 1844 and 1862. The Medical Officer of Clerkenwell wrote of the district:

> 'There are some good houses, where some good families were brought up, where they used to keep their carriages; they retire into the country, and those houses are let to a family in each floor; there is a continual outgo of good people and a continual in-come of working people.' [8]

The Medical Officer of Islington said in 1865 that there was in the area 'an excess of Law Clerks, Commercial Clerks, Schoolmasters, Printers, Goldsmiths, Jewellers, Watchmakers, Butchers, Carpenters, Joiners, Plasterers and Bricklayers' adding that in the surrounding areas 'we have a slight excess of Schoolmistresses, Dressmakers and Milliners, Washerwomen and Domestic Servants'. That the area was becoming rough was conceded by Charles Dickens Jr. who said that the area had acquired a reputation for cheap lodgings, and that High Street and Upper Street had grown to be amongst the noisiest and least agreeable throughfares in London[9]. That the area was in parts becoming desperately poor is indicated by the fact that in 1861 a soup kitchen, situated in Cobham Row near Clerkenwell Green, served soup and bread 8,500 times in ten days—a clientele as large as that visiting the theatre nearby.

It was not however the declining wealth of the neighbourhood which caused Phelps increasing disquiet in the last years of his management—

THEATRE ROYAL, HAYMARKET.

Amateur Performance

IN AID OF

THE FUND FOR THE ENDOWMENT OF A PERPETUAL CURATORSHIP OF
SHAKESPEARE'S HOUSE,

TO BE ALWAYS HELD BY SOME ONE DISTINGUISHED IN LITERATURE, AND MORE ESPECIALLY IN DRAMATIC LITERATURE; THE
PROFITS OF WHICH, IT IS THE INTENTION OF THE SHAKESPEARE HOUSE COMMITTEE TO KEEP ENTIRELY SEPARATE
FROM THE FUND NOW RAISING FOR THE PURCHASE OF THE HOUSE.

On Monday Evening, May 15th, 1848, will be presented,

SHAKESPEARE'S COMEDY OF

THE MERRY WIVES OF WINDSOR.

Sir John Falstaff	Mr. Mark Lemon.
Fenton	Mr. Charles Romer.
Shallow, a Country Justice	Mr. Charles Dickens.
Slender, Cousin to Shallow	Mr. John Leech.
Mr. Ford } Two Gentlemen dwelling at Windsor	{ Mr. John Forster.
Mr. Page }	{ Mr. Frank Stone.
Sir Hugh Evans, a Welsh Parson	Mr. G. H. Lewes.
Dr. Caius, a French Physician	Mr. Dudley Costello.
Host of the Garter Inn	Mr. Frederick Dickens.
Bardolph }	{ Mr. Cole.
Pistol } Followers of Falstaff	{ Mr. George Cruikshank.
Nym }	{ Mr. Augustus Dickens.
Robin }	{ Miss Robins.
Simple, Servant to Slender	Mr. Augustus Egg.
Rugby, Servant to Dr. Caius	Mr. Eaton.
Mrs. Ford	Miss Fortescue.
Mrs. Page	Miss Kenworthy.
Mrs. Anne Page, her Daughter, in love with Fenton . . .	Miss Anne Romer.
Mrs. Quickly, Servant to Dr. Caius	Mrs. Cowden Clarke.

The Costumes (of the period of Henry IV.) by Messrs. Nathan, of Titchbourne Street.

To conclude with Mrs. Inchbald's Farce of

ANIMAL MAGNETISM.

The Doctor . . . Mr. Charles Dickens.		Jeffrey . . . . Mr. George Cruikshank.	
La Fleur . . . Mr. Mark Lemon.		Constance . . . Miss Anne Romer.	
The Marquis de Lancy . Mr. John Leech.		Lisette . . . . Miss Fortescue.	

THE BAND WILL PERFORM

Previous to the Comedy	Shakespearian Overture	Sir H. R. Bishop.
Between the Acts	{ Fantasia introducing the Favourite Melodies of } the Fourteenth and Fifteenth Centuries	T. German Reed.
Previous to the Farce	The Overture to Pré aux Clercs	Herold.

. The Doors will be opened at half-past Six, and the performance will commence at half-past Seven precisely, by which time
it is requested that the whole of the Company may be seated.

Directors of General Arrangements—Mr. John Payne Collier, Mr. Charles Knight, Mr. Peter Cunningham,
AND THE LONDON SHAKESPEARE HOUSE COMMITTEE.

Stage Manager—Mr. Charles Dickens.

EVENING DRESS IN ALL PARTS OF THE HOUSE.

Dickens' 'Amateur Theatricals' made considerable inroads on the professional theatres' audience. Note that evening dress was required for all parts of the house.

42

his audience by then was not drawn primarily from Islington—but growing competition that he was ill-equipped to meet. First, there was in North London a growing amateur movement. Before the beginning of his management J. G. Burton listed the following private theatres which regularly presented amateur performances, all between the centres of London and Sadler's Wells:

> Berwick Street, Theatre, High Holborn.
> Bologna's Theatre, Strand.
> Bury Street Theatre.
> Chivers Rooms, Strand.
> Coal Hole, Fountain Court, Strand.
> Gloster Street Theatre, Gloucester Street.
> Kean's Head, Russell Court.
> Minor Theatre, Catherine Street.
> Mitchell's Rooms, Portsmouth Street.
> Pymm's Theatre, Wilson Street. [10]

And during Phelps' management the amateur movement, led, irritatingly enough, by many of his own supporters, Charles Dickens in particular, flourished. Performances such as Dickens' presentation of an amateur company at the Haymarket, in 1848, playing *The Merry Wives of Windsor*, or his 1851 presentation of Lytton's *Not So Bad As We Seem* to the Queen and her Consort at Devonshire House, at times vied with Phelps for the loyalty of London's *literati*, and were a regular, and increasing, feature of fashionable London life in the 1850s and 60s.

Of more rapid growth was a different and stronger competition. From 1860, when the Empire opened in the High Street, with a capacity of 1,500, Islington rapidly became a centre of the music hall. In 1861 Deacon's Music Hall, with a capacity of 800, opened in Myddleton Square. In 1862, the best-known of them, Collins' Music Hall, seating 600, opened on Islington Green. Meanwhile the old Alexandra Theatre in Highbury Park was being rebuilt, with a planned capacity of 1,900, and between the larger fish were scattered many smaller fry; 32 public houses in Islington successfully applied for entertainments licences between 1855 and 1862, and for a period Islington's 'golden mile' rivalled similar areas near the Strand and in Hoxton as an entertainment centre.

Amateur productions, and the early music halls, had in common certain advantages. They were not hampered by many of the wasteful managerial traditions of the straight theatre—they did not have to yield seats regularly to the theatre owners for example, nor give free

43

'orders' to members of the legitimate 'acting profession'. Production and stage management costs too were in the case of the amateurs minimal, and in the case of music hall, very much lower than those for a fully fitted-up production. They did not therefore come to rely increasingly upon the patronage of an advantaged and monied class, but could, charging lower admission prices, recoup expenditure from the patronage of the popular audience. For Phelps the case was different. His productions were expensive by the custom of the day; *Pericles*, for example, cost £1,000 to stage. He was made by the terms of his lease to yield to the Proprietors two private boxes at each performance, and 'the right to introduce 20 visitors before the curtain on the night of every Performance, except on Benefit nights, and also to introduce a limited number of persons on the Free List'. He was obliged to cut further into his possible income by the regular granting of benefit performances to his fellow players and colleagues (from which they took all profit) and, as we have seen, he felt he could not raise prices. The only obvious solution was to move to a larger theatre, and to take his audience with him.

We know from May Phelps and Forbes-Robertson that at least twice during those last years he considered moving to a bigger venue[11]. Had he done so, it is likely that he *would* have carried his audience with him, for Phelps is properly seen not as an Islington missionary, but as a shrewd London manager who demonstrated that, had later managers chosen to move in that direction, a successful London theatre could be located in an area quite different from the fashionable centre. Indeed had he moved, his influence might have been greater still, for he might have demonstrated that the best managerial instincts are not always those which tend towards the promotion of the small-scale and exclusive. As it was, his reappearance as an actor in central London demonstrated that he retained both the affection of his North London followers and his pleasure in the big and popular. In 1866, when he opened in *King John* at Drury Lane, he wrote to his wife:

'Every thing was right last night. The house was splendid. £50 more than any opening night yet. My reception lasted between two and three minutes. My voice was in fine condition and I never acted better. The Sadler's Wells lot were all there.' [12]

Of course things were now reverting to the pre-1843 way. The 'Sadler's Wells lot' were coming in as suppliants to the shrine of the 'centre', not, as had incredibly been the case for eighteen years receiving visitors from central London in their own, good, suburban theatre.

44

4
The Refinement of the Bancrofts 1865-1885

One point must strike all in connection with Bancroft's career - before he left the Haymarket, at the age of forty-four, he was the most senior theatrical manager of London. In conjunction with that gifted lady who was the genius of English comedy, he popularised a system of management which has dominated our stage ever since.

Henry Irving 1900

Sir Squire and Lady Bancroft had the most profound influence upon the form and character of the West End theatre by virtue of two periods of management. The first, begun by Lady Bancroft when she was known still by her unmarried name, Marie Wilton, was at a small theatre in Tottenham Street, which she renamed the Prince of Wales's; it began in 1865 and lasted fifteen years. The second, a joint management throughout, was when the Bancrofts ran the Haymarket theatre from 1860 to 1865. In 1865 they retired from management, and virtually withdrew from the profession, having made a net personal profit of £180,000 from 20 years' work, and with a considerable reputation for having 'refined' the London stage. In his survey of the nineteenth century, *The Life of a Century* Edwin Hodder remarked with approval that 'of all that has been accomplished in the way of rendering the English stage elegant and refined, both before and behind the curtain, the Bancrofts have been the pioneers.' [1]

There is some justice in this. Undoubtedly they treated their comparatively small company of actors well. They abolished the humiliating tradition whereby actors had to queue in semi-public for their weekly wage, and the wages themselves improved steadily. During their management John Hare's salary, for example, rose from £2 to £20 a week, and George Honey, when re-engaged during the Haymarket management to play the same part in Robertson's *Caste* that he had formerly played at the Prince of Wales's for £18, had his weekly salary raised to £60. Although they rarely attempted the large scale and complex architectural settings of some of their fellow actor managers, their scenes were well-made, detailed and practical, and the furnishings and fittings were, as befitted their 'cup and saucer comedies', tasteful and realistic. The acting style which they created with their companies was genteel and deft, purged of over-emphatic theatrical mannerisms, and reflecting the constraint and manners of their middle class audiences. The auditoriums too were increasingly refined, reflecting in layout and decoration the prevailing notions of good taste held by their high-ranking clientele.

Such refinement was however achieved at a high cost. The success of the Prince of Wales's management was a success of a small theatre which relied upon the regular attendance of a privileged audience able to pay much higher admission prices than had hitherto been charged in London, but one which excluded by its charges and by its social ambience a considerable portion of the capital's potential theatre-goers. It meant that the managers who controlled the West End in the following decades became convinced that it was better business to cater for a privileged coterie who could pay higher prices than to build and run larger popular theatres. Equally damaging, by creating that particular social milieu in their theatres, the Bancrofts convinced their fellow managers that a refined and influential audience of the genteel sort considerably enhanced the managers' own social standing. By their success, and by the decisive alteration which they made all at once to the artistic, administrative and social nature of theatre management, the Bancrofts may be said to have significantly formed the character of West End theatre.

That they were conscious of their role may be seen by the immense pains they took to record and justify details of their management. Although it is common for West End impresarios to write their memoirs, no other manager has approached the detail, the high seriousness and the prolongued justifications which the Bancrofts published after their retirement. Their first substantial publication, a two volume memoir called *On and Off the Stage*, was published a year after their retirement in 1886. In 1909 they retold the story of their management 'with that greater freedom that is born of the lapse of time', under the title of *Recollections of Sixty Years*, and in 1911 brought out a cheap edition of the same book, which runs to 475 pages. In 1925

Squire Bancroft, who survived his wife, published a book of essays, *Empty Chairs*, in which he returns again to a lengthy eulogy upon his wife's integrity and talent. One effect of this has been that by seeming to give so generously of information about their management, the Bancrofts' actions are scrutinised less critically by nineteenth century researchers than are other major West End managers, and their motives are frequently taken as being all that the Bancrofts said they were. Thus Frances Donaldson, in *The Actor Managers*, says that 'Bancroft combined the sure instinct of the born moneymaker with the genuine humanity of the reformer'[2]. It is the kind of epithet that Bancroft would have liked, but as we shall shortly see, the facts do not always support the second part of the judgement. It was not the unanimous view of his contemporaries that he was motivated by genuine humanity.

Marie Wilton was born in 1839, one of the six daughters of a failed travelling actor, Robert Wilton. She was a child actress, brought out very young, making her first appearance in London, at the Lyceum theatre, on September 15, 1856, and for nine years enjoyed a growing reputation as a player in farce and burlesque at the Haymarket, Strand, Adelphi and St. James's theatres. The poverty and raffishness of the popular theatre seem however equally to have repelled her, as she makes clear in a memoir of her father:

'My father, who was much older than my mother, eloped with her when he was a travelling actor. His rashness cost them dear; their lot for many years was little more than toil, anxiety and care. Dazzled by the eternal glitter of the stage, my father went his way, building castles in the air and living in dreamland. Having been brought up in luxury and refinement they felt their changed condition keenly, and often in later life have recalled to me stories of my childhood and events in our early days, which have carried me painfully back to the past.' [3]

Her childhood and past often pained her, as did her early association with burlesque, although she conceded it had an early value for her as a training. Since those days however, she remarked tartly, 'although burlesque may not have fallen off, perhaps some of the dresses have; many of which might be described as beginning too late and ending too soon'[4]. Lady Bancroft had all of the prudeur of the Victorian middle class.

In 1865 her brother-in-law offered to lend her £1,000 in order to set up in theatre management, and, in spite of the fact that it was in an 'awful' neighbourhood, at a great distance from 'the fashionable world', she took the Queen's Theatre in Tottenham Street at a weekly rental of £20. The loan was banked in her name on January 21, and she entered into partnership with H. J. Byron, agreeing with him that she should be paid £20 a week from receipts (a half of which should go towards repaying the loan) and he should be paid £10 a week, and indemnified from any further financial risk. The theatre, renamed the Prince Of Wales's, by her wish, opened on April 15, after some £850 had been spent from the capital loan in its redecoration.

Not only the change of title, but the form the redecoration took, showed the new management's intentions. On an early visit to the theatre Lady Bancroft had noticed the noisy behaviour of the local audience with some distaste. People were 'devouring oranges', 'drinking ginger beer' and trying to calm crying children by smacking them to be quiet. The auditorium was uncarpeted, the crude wooden seating uncomfortable, and admission she noted was only a shilling. By contrast when it reopened under her management it was carpeted, curtained and the light blue stall seats had lace antimacassars over them. She was proud of the changes:

> 'This was the first time such things had ever been seen in a theatre. The pampered audiences of the present day, accustomed to the modern luxurious playhouses, little know of how much my modest undertaking was the pioneer, and would hardly credit that a carpet in the stalls was, until then, unknown.' [5]

At first the price of admission to the tasteful new stalls was 6/-, but shortly after her marriage to Squire Bancroft in 1867, when he had joined her in management, not only was the auditorium's 'prettiness' all destroyed but, as Lady Bancroft wryly notes, such decoration was 'prosaically and profitably replaced by extra stalls', which then cost 7/-. Seven years later the stall price had been raised to 10/-. The original £1,000 loan was repaid in 1866, and with the accumulating profits, a separate opening to the enlarged new stall area was built, together with a Royal entrance, and a new tier of private boxes, each of which contained handsome fans made of peacocks' feathers, attached to the box by a gilt chain. The local population who had, Lady Bancroft remarks with pride, 'never seen such a display of carriages' as that which attended her opening night, must plainly have lost any belief that their local theatre had anything more to do with their lives.

It was of course not only the admission prices that deterred the

48

humbler citizens of the area from joining the fashionable audience, but the timing and nature of the programme. The Bancrofts did away with the custom of charging 'half-price after nine o'clock' when the after-pieces were played, and replaced that kind of programme with a single play, commencing at eight o'clock, which was, as Squire Bancroft asserts, 'a thing unknown before'. It was thus very much more difficult for manual workers to go at all, particularly as a change of clothing would have been necessary, as their work did not finish in time. Moreover the programme itself was, in content and style, of particular appeal to a middle class audience. After H. J. Byron had ended his partnership with Lady Bancroft in 1867, uneasy with her decision to abandon the widely popular burlesques in which she had made her name, the theatre was largely sustained by a succession of comedies by T. W. Robertson; *Caste* in 1867, *Play* in 1868, *School* and *Home* in 1869, interspersed with revivals of *Ours* and *Society*. Their major significance lies in the detail with which they were staged, at their best mirroring middle class life. The working class characters are in contrast coarsely drawn, and the imperialism, as Professor Wilson Knight points out in *The Golden Labyrinth*, is crude. [6]

The programme, its timing, the cost of admission and of course the manners and dress of the fashionable and influential audience were all calculated to deter the ordinary citizens from the neighbourhood, and were indeed equally likely to deter that broader following that had enjoyed Lady Bancroft's performances as a star of burlesque. The Bancrofts sought unashamedly to attract the rich, the titled, the fashionable and the respectable artistic and literary figures of the city to their theatre. It was their attendance which made the theatre, quite quickly, in Ellen Terry's phrase, 'the most fashionable in London', and it was their approval which the Bancrofts did not hesitate to publish. The managerial aims are made explicit in a revealing paragraph in which Bancroft looks back on the Prince of Wales's after they had relinquished management there:

'Often in the twilight of afteryears, when it was closed and deserted, have we pensively gazed upon the dilapidated, crumbling, once brilliant little theatre, and wondered if the past was but a dream. Could it be true that Dickens and Lytton had so often sat there to listen to us, with hundreds and hundreds of the greatest in the land? Could it be that actors, and painters, and authors, since known to all the world, had fought for places in the pit? Could it be that we once had difficulty to find a seat there for Gladstone, and had listened to an ovation given within its walls to Beaconsfield? Could it have been under that mournful-looking porch that the constant stream of youth and age, of beauty, wit, and wealth, had flowed for so many years?' [7]

There is never any question of attempting—as Samuel Phelps had attempted in his first months at Sadler's Wells—to attract a local audience. The uncouth clientele who so revolted Lady Bancroft on her first visit to the unrefined theatre lived still in an unfashionable twilight, untouched by the 'glittering success' of what had been their local theatre.

Already, in 1879, Bancroft had 'vague ideas of some day retiring from management'. He had made already a modest fortune (he was able, when he and his wife moved to manage the Haymarket theatre, to draw £20,000 from the 'savings' they had made from their work at the Prince of Wales's), and it is likely that he had in mind a further ten years' work at most which would enable them to live in the style to which they had accustomed themselves; she driving in the fashionable London parks, he a prominent figure in the cultural establishment at the Garrick Club and the Athenaeum. However in that year Bancroft learned that a rival, Hare, had joined with the Kendals to take the St. James's Theatre, in the fashionable heart of London, and in the centre of what was becoming the lucrative West End. 'So powerful a trio as himself with the Kendals, in a new and better-placed house, rendered handsome and up-to-date, gave me pause'[8]. He at once made an offer to the lessee of the Haymarket, J. S. Clarke, and with remarkable speed, arranged to leave the Prince of Wales's and move to the Haymarket theatre, for a maximum period of ten years.

There is good reason for supposing that Bancroft's account of the reasons for the move is not the whole truth. Certainly Hare and the Kendals would provide strong opposition, but the audience for the well-dressed and fashionable drama was expanding. None of the nine new theatres built since the opening of the Prince of Wales's was in financial difficulty. The great expansion of the popular press, the rapid development of the railways and city transport system, and the rising population of the city itself would all seem to indicate that an established management like the Bancrofts had no need to fear any falling away of receipts.

It was however the weakening of a *social* position that Bancroft feared. His position in Victorian society rested upon the carefully fostered belief that in every way he had 'refined' the theatre. He was now threatened, not only with what seemed like equally stylish counterparts operating in a more glamorous area, but with the disturbing new managerial style of Henry Irving, who had commenced his own managerial career at the Lyceum theatre at the beginning of 1879, and who was already drawing much fashionable attention. It was a more flamboyant and coarser style, but the danger was that Irving could lead the emergent Victorian theatre into less refined and more populist realms. Although professing eternal friendship for Irving in his writing Bancroft loses few opportunities to remind his readers that Irving's cultured veneer was hard-won:

'Although denied, by the accident of life, the advantages of a first-class education, Irving possessed the knowledge and the learning which schools and colleges may fail to teach; and certainly, in his later years, he would have graced, in manner and aspect, any position to which he might have been called. The refinement of his appearance grew to be remarkable—the Church or the Bench, equally with literature or science, might with pride in that regard have claimed him as a chief. This personal attribute only came to him towards the autumn of his life, which it so adorned. Truth to tell, in the early part of his career he had but little, if any, of it. In those distant days there was indeed a smack of the country actor in his appearance; and, if it is not profanity to utter the thought, even a suggestion of a type immortalised by Dickens.' [9]

Certainly he does not describe Irving as a possible rival, but it is hard to believe that the sudden success of a poorly-educated, crudely mannered and provincial actor did not privately worry Bancroft rather more than the appearance of another company adopting the theatrical style which the Bancrofts themselves had nurtured for the London audience.

A second reason for the move, which Bancroft does not directly discuss, was that the Prince of Wales's theatre was scarcely safe and would, in all probability, have needed considerably more than the £20,000 which was invested in the Haymarket theatre for extensive structural alterations, repairs and the necessary refurbishing and redecoration. The Lord Chamberlain's department had begun annual inspections of London's theatres in 1855, and an official, accompanied by a surveyor, would inspect each theatre with particular attention to 1) Means of egress in case of fire, 2) Good ventilation, 3) Means of extinguishing fire, 4) Safe hanging of chandeliers, and 5) Cleanliness and order of the building. Managers would after each inspection receive letters telling them of matters to be put right. In the 1860s the inspectors began to pay further attention to 1) Protection of footlights, 2) Wing lights being raised four feet from the stage floor, and 3) Making dresses of uninflammable material. The Bancroft management undoubtedly received their share of criticism, and Bancroft says that they 'were annually reminded' of the Theatre's many drawbacks 'when the house was inspected by the Lord Chamberlain's representatives.' [10]

Soon however a much more severe inspection was begun, and the fabric of theatre buildings subjected to a much more serious examination each year, following the *Metropolis Management and Building Acts* of 1878. Some of the theatres were closed, and those existing subjected to a much more devastating critique. It is likely that at the time he made the move to the Haymarket theatre Bancroft was well aware that a very large sum would have to be spent on the Prince of Wales's to make it conform to new regulations, so large in fact that the alterations to the Haymarket would be cheaper and—given the Haymarket's increased (though still modest) size—better exploit their known patrons. In the event the Prince of Wales's theatre was declared unsafe following the Bancrofts' departure, was refused a licence in 1882, and until 1903 (when it was totally rebuilt) was used as a Salvation Army Hostel for the St. Pancras area.

In 1879 the management could hardly have been worried over the scale of their box-office receipts. The Prince of Wales's was (Figure 2) overall the most expensive theatre in London. It was drawing excellent houses, and the **maximum** nightly receipts were:

	£	s.	d.	
Stalls (143)	71	10	0	at 10/-.
Pit (85)	10	12	6	at 2/6.
Circles (134)	29	4	0	at 6/-. 4/-. 3/-.
Boxes (142 seats)	50	8	0	at £2.2s. and £1.1s.
Amphitheatre	2	10	0	at 1/-.
Total	164	4	6	

As Lady Bancroft later said that 'the nightly expenses at the old Prince of Wales's theatre never exceeded £70', it is a reasonable conclusion that a week of full houses for six performances would have yielded a gross profit in excess of £500. Allowing for the costs of new productions, and the outlay on maintenance and on meeting the Lord

Figure 2
Prices in London's theatres 1879

	Stalls	Dress Circle	Upper Circle	Pit
Adelphi	10s 6d	5s	3s	2s
Alhambra	6s	None	None	2s
Brittania	1s	None	1s	6d
Court	10s	6s	4s	2s
Criterion	7s 6d & 10s	5s	4s	2s
Duke's	7s 6d	5s	3s	1s 6d
East London	1s	1s 6d	1s	6d
Elephant and Castle	2s	2s	1s	6d
Folly	10s 6d	5s	3s	2s
Gaiety	10s	5s	3s	2s
Globe	10s 6d	5s	4s	2s
Grecian	3s	1s 6d	1s	6d
Haymarket	10s*	5s	3s	?s
Imperial	7s	5s	3s	2s
Lyceum	10s	6s	3s	2s
Marylebone	2s	1s 6d	1s	6d
Olympic	7s 6d	5s	4s	2s
Opera Comique	10s	2s 6d	None	None
Park	4s	3s	2s	1s
Pavilion	1s	1s 6d	None	6d
Philharmonic	3s	None	None	1s
Prince of Wales's	10s	6s	4s	2s 6d
Princess's	7s	5s	3s	2s
Royalty	10s	3s	None	2s
Standard	4s	3s	2s	6d
Strand	10s	3s	None	2s
Surrey	5s	3s	2s	6d
Vaudeville	10s	6s	3s	2s 6d
Victoria	1s	1s 6d	1s	1s

* These were the prices charged in the building before Bancroft's management and before the alterations.

The present Haymarket Theatre (right) replaced the old one (left) in 1821. Shortly afterwards the old Haymarket was demolished. However, when Bancroft took the lease on the new Haymarket in 1880, it too had fallen into some disrepair.

Chamberlain's requirements, it is still a fair assumption that at least a third of their eventual net profit of £180,000 had been made *before* the Bancrofts left the Prince of Wales's.

When he took the Haymarket theatre Bancroft noted that it was 'greatly in need of rebuilding, and certainly of re-furbishing'. His rebuilding and renovation however took an unexpected course. Although the existing capacity of the theatre was twice that of the Prince of Wales's, and the existing seated capacity almost 1,000, he decided to restructure the auditorium so that the pit—the most famous in London, whose adherents had a reputation for good behaviour and good judgement—could be done away with, and stalls substituted in their place. There was no pressing financial need for this. Although the investment in the theatre was £20,000, and nightly running costs rose at once to £100 and later to £120, the existing layout of the theatre would have yielded a satisfactory profit. Bancroft however insisted that the change was financially imperative, and saw the change as exhibiting the qualities of his own managerial courage and leadership:

> 'The pit had long lost, in most West End theatres, the possibility of being the support it used to prove; the managers, with ourselves as their leaders, having, row by row, robbed it of its power, and made the stalls instead their 'backbone'. This grew to be pre-eminently the case with our own management, which, owing to the large salaries paid to actors and the expenses of production, could not have endured without the high-priced admission which I had the courage to inaugurate.' [11]

In an attempt to forestall criticism from the pittites, and from that section of the profession that doubted his motives, he issued before the opening night a public explanation:

> 'As some disappointment may be felt at the abolition of the pit, Mr and Mrs Bancroft deem it necessary to explain the alteration. With the present expense of a first-class theatre it is impossible to give up the floor of the house—its most remunerative portion—to low-priced seats, and the management, being unwilling to place any part of the audience in close and confined space under the balcony, the only alternative was to allot the frequenters of the pit the tier usually devoted to the upper boxes and now called the second circle.' [12]

The appeal however fell on deaf ears. The opening night was checked by a riot in favour of the restoration of the pit, and the theatrical profession was sharply divided as to the merits or otherwise of Bancroft's decision.

It remains true however that had Bancroft left the pit in its former position, he would have taken sufficient from good houses to meet running costs, repay his investment and make a reasonable profit. We know that the annual rental for the theatre was £5,000. It we spread the costs of repayment of the £20,000 invested over five years and, in addition, allow the Bancrofts an annual profit of £5,000, then we are looking for an income, to balance the budget, of £14,000 a year. If we take an average running cost of £110 a night, and assume an average of 6 performances a week over a 40 week season, then the total running costs are £26,400. (As most of the productions were revivals, we shall ignore production costs; as the theatre was newly rebuilt and refurbished we shall also ignore additional costs of alteration and maintenance). In broad terms therefore the annual outgoings were as follows:

		£
Rental		5,000
Conversion costs		4,000
Running costs		26,400
Profit		5,000
	Total	40,400

In order for him to reach that figure, each performance during a 40 week season should have yielded an average income of £168.6s.8d.

Ignoring for the moment any income to be derived from the pit/stall area on the ground floor, the *remainder* of the auditorium would yield more than this minimal figure when attendance was at maximum;

1st Circle (187)	56	2	0	at 6/-
2nd Circle (174)	26	2	0	at 3/-
Gallery (244)	12	4	0	at 1/-
Balcony (172)	43	0	0	at 5/-
Boxes (132 seats)	69	6	0	at £3.3s and £2.2s
Total	206	14	0	

If however there were a 60% attendance, and the remainder of the auditorium yielded only £124.0s.6d., then a 60% attendance, at 3/-, in the former 500-strong pit would have still brought in £45, making the total £169.0s.6d.

Had the Bancrofts therefore been satisfied with a repayment of their investment within five years, and a further net profit of £5,000 per annum, they could have continued to run the theatre with its pit—even playing very well below their reasonable expectations, at 60%! However the increased number of stall seats, 249, sold at 10/- each, made a profound difference. A 60% capacity of those yielded an additional £30.18s.10d. profit each evening giving the Bancrofts (6 performances × 30 weeks × £30.18s.10d.) an additional profit in excess of £7,000, making a total, for each season, of £12,000.

Such figures for income ignore the additional revenue from programme, bar, and cloakrooms, but even so when we begin to look at the likely profit from a more reasonable 75% average attendance, we can begin to arrive at a judgement over Bancroft's insistence that it was *impossible* to give up the floor of the house to the pit. For a 75% attendance, making the same broad assumptions, the nightly income is £248.14s.0d., which, with the notional profit of £5,000 already allowed for, makes an annual profit in excess of £24,000. Bearing in mind the kinds of figures we are given from profits for individual productions, and knowing, as we do, that although the Haymarket was not always as full as the 'thronged' Prince of Wales's had been, it is reasonable to assume then, even allowing for the 'repayment' of the £20,000 they had invested, that the Bancrofts made something little short of £120,000 from their five seasons at the Haymarket, which was added to the £60,000 they had made at their former theatre. After the event, and forgetting his claims that the abolition of the pit was not simply profitable, but 'necessary', Bancroft wrote smugly that, 'The large profits made by us at the Haymarket were, I think, as little suspected as known'. [13]

Whether they suspected or not, many of his fellow professionals were sceptical of his explanations; some appeared not only to resent the change in the nature of London theatre-going which the abolition of the pit represented, but seemed to hint at least that they suspected that financial rather than humanitarian motives were at the root of it. Many of the arguments were marshalled together in a lengthy symposium *Is the Pit an Institution or an Excrescence?* which appeared in *The Theatre* 1st March 1880. Firstly the argument, presented by Frank Marshall, that the pittites were simply a better and more responsive audience than the socialising groups that frequented the stalls of London theatres:

'The cheaper price is paid by those who come solely to enjoy the entertainment, and therefore devote their whole attention to what is being said or done on the stage, and not, as their more fashionable rivals, to what is being done or said around them.' [14]

More telling is the lengthy argument by the Editor, Scott, which is hostile to the Bancrofts, seeing in the replacement of the popular area by a fashionable stalls a 'reform' that 'is of far deeper moment than is generally believed to be the case'. He argues that 'the ten shilling stalls are the falsest of all false economies', and continues:

'If this were only a commercial question and nothing else, as some people imagine it is, there would be really nothing more to say about it. The management at the Haymarket can do what it likes with its own property, can paint its walls sky-blue or pea-green, or turn it topsy turvy if it chooses—no one doubts it; but I must protest against the assertion that it is only to be argued by those who loll in the new stalls and not those excluded from the old pit. As to Mr Bancroft's figures, I have nothing to do with them except to doubt them. 'When has the theatre ever paid?' he asked. I am informed by the very best authority that it has paid over and over again with a pit, when the plays and the acting have been of the first class . . . Mr and Mrs Bancroft ought to be at the head of the first company of comedians in the country, and by that I mean a company acceptable to the public at large and not only to the upholders of a fashionable and fastidious exclusiveness.' [15]

Yet Scott's sarcasm was to no avail, for a fashionable exclusiveness, allied to profit, precisely summarised the Bancrofts' intentions. Evening dress became *de rigeur* for the Haymarket stalls as, towards the end, it had been usual at the Prince of Wales's; the audience saw much of the old repertoire safely through again, framed now by an expensive proscenium arch of gold. As Henry James remarked, London's drama was now 'not a popular amusement'. In the year of the Haymarket's reopening under the Bancrofts he deplored:

'The necessity of dining earlier than usual and of dressing as if for a private entertainment. These things testify to the theatre's being a fashion among a certain class, and the last luxury of a few, rather than taking its place in the common habits of the people, as it does in France.' [16]

He found the new Haymarket comfortable, but mocks the tired repertoire which the Bancrofts put forward as entertainment for their well-mannered audiences; the plays of Robertson he dismisses as 'infantile'.

In one sense of course it might be just to call the entirety of the management infantile. The 'refinement' of a society's manners and

Figure 3

London Theatre-Building during the Bancrofts' Managements: 1865-1885

1867	Holborn Theatre	Capacity	980
1868	Globe, Strand	,,	1,000
1868	Gaiety	,,	1,126
1869	Charing Cross (afterwards Toole's)	,,	650
1870	Court, Chelsea	,,	600
1870	Vaudeville	,,	1,000
1870	Opera Comique	,,	862
1874	Criterion	,,	675
1876	Imperial	,,	1,293
1881	Savoy	,,	1,300
1881	Comedy	,,	1,055
1882	Avenue (afterwards the Playhouse)	,,	1,500
1882	Novelty (afterwards the Kingsway)	,,	675
1883	Prince's (afterwards the new Prince of Wales's)	,,	960

(Erroneously, Bancroft says that in 1867 the Queen's theatre was opened. In fact it was **re**-opened in that year. Having been built before the decades of the Bancrofts' influence, in 1850, it belongs to an earlier managerial tradition, that of provision on a larger scale. It accommodated 4,000.)

mores can mean that elaborate and expensive rituals become a substitute for direct experience, rather than an achievement of it. There is certainly a childishness about the growing 'refinement' of the Bancrofts' audience; the separate doors for stalls entrants, the elaborate dressing up, the codewords in the new theatrical language of refinement, the general air of jealous exclusivity, are more usually associated with the secret societies of childhood than with the adult behaviour of a 'general public'. Plays reflect the audience, and audience the plays. There is a ritual here; well-known actors in well-tried plays in a style that flattered but did not extend the appreciation of the audience.

Overall the influence of the Bancrofts was very great. In some details they were innovators; they brought a new dignity to theatre management and treated their actors better than most managements had previously done. Their own social and financial success however gave momentum to another innovation—the axiom that refinement of the theatre art was inextricably bound up with the wooing of a refined and fashionable audience. As Figure 3 shows, they also gave considerable impetus to the notion that the proper way to run a London theatre was with a small auditorium.

They also decisively altered the financial balance of theatre production by playing work that was small-cast, but with well-paid actors. Thus in budgetary terms their on-stage practice once more curiously reflected their practice in the auditorium. A smaller group of well-paid actors was paid for by fewer but much more highly-priced seats; on both sides of the curtain their influence was to encourage exclusivity.

5
Entertainment in the West End

I'd take her to the Aquarium, I'd take her to the Zoo:
I'd take her to the Waxwork show, and the Crystal Palace too.
Oh yes, if only she'd be true, it would fill me with delight,
And I'd take her to the music-hall - Every Saturday Night!

Music Hall song 1860s

An examination of the Bancrofts' managements show that the 'refinement' of London theatre sought as deliberately to exclude the poorer classes as to attract a society audience. Within the profession there was some disquiet about this. An anxious editorial in *The Theatre* of September 1878, worried that the theatre was losing its popular base, points out that only the well-to-do could then afford the fashionable theatres. A man with an income of 'something under four hundred a year' for example (considerably higher than an ordinary working class wage) would now find that two seats for himself and his wife in the dress circle, together with a shilling booking fee, 6d. for a programme, 6d. each for cloakroom facilities and travel and refreshment, would leave him little change from a sovereign:

'The class of playgoers kept away by the considerations we have named is, we contend, the very one which in the long run will most certainly and most seriously be missed. It includes the backbone of the educated and taste-possessing people for whose return to the play-house we have for so long been hoping against hope. It includes professional men, and artists, and authors, and students of every kind except the small minority which has made out of art, or science, or study, an income equal to that of the uncultured tradesman.' [1]

Few contemporary observers however regretted the absence of the working class minority, who were generally assumed to be not only uneducated and uncultured, but by their base natures unreachable by the emerging West End theatre. Indeed later commentators have usually gone further and assumed that the working classes were best excluded. George Rowell's comment on the emergence of the Music Hall in *The Victorian Theatre*, for example, betrays a comfortable assumption that the working class theatre audience was inevitably violent and undiscriminating:

'In particular the evolution of the Music Hall at this time began to draw off the violent element in the audience. By its transformation from the semi-secret haunt of the raffish man-about-town into the popular resort of the working man, providing both drink and entertainment, the Music Hall took over one of the chief functions of the mid Victorian theatre. The way was thus cleared . . . for a smaller, more discriminating audience.' [2]

The new music halls were certainly attracting a large audience. Although the first hall had not been established in the centre of London until 1861, when Charles Morton opened the Oxford, in Oxford Street, by 1870 nine major music halls were running in the heart of the city. They were the London Pavilion, Leicester Square; the Sun Music Hall, Knightsbridge; Raglan Music Hall, Bloomsbury; Sam Collins Music Hall; Marylebone Music Hall; Alhambra Palace, Leicester Square; Winchester Music Hall in Southwark Bridge Road; Middlesex Music Hall, Drury Lane and Gatti's Hall of Varieties, Westminster Bridge Road. More than thirty other major venues were within comfortable reach of the centre, including the particular concentrations in Hoxton and Islington, and including such well-known names as the Metropolitan, Edgware Road, Forester's Grand Music Hall at Mile-end and the Eastern Music Hall at Limehouse. In general their capacities were higher than the theatres being built in the West End at the time, and by the end of the 1870s the Music Hall audience was probably already larger than the West End one.

It has become something of a critical commonplace to say that their audiences were noisy, undiscriminating and generally rowdy, and thus to justify the increasing separation and refinement of the theatres following the Bancroft style. Such a blanket opinion is however unjustified. First, because audiences at the West End theatres were by no means well-behaved all the time; in spite of the pressures of a new social comformity audiences in the straight theatre, from Bancroft's Haymarket opening to the rowdy behaviour in the West End on boat race night between the wars, could behave riotously on occasion. Second, because there is much evidence that even in its earliest forms, the music hall usually played to an orderly gathering. Samuel McKechnie, whose survey *Popular Entertainments Through the Ages* is still regarded as being one of the best and most comprehensive surveys of the field, quotes an early description of a music hall which gives a useful corrective:

'The audience is composed of working-class people of both sexes, most of them below the age of twenty and some of them mere children. They enter through the door of a shop, and in return for their penny each of them receives from the girl a square tin check. Then they pass into the dark vestibule which is lit by only a single spur of gas projecting from the plaster on the wall . . . Everything is so much in order as regards decency that the two sexes sit in different parts of the hall.' [*3*]

The mention of the extreme youth of the audience is interesting. It is, in the 1870s and 1880s, a common observation. In *Ally Sloper's Half Holiday* in 1888, George R. Sims describes a packed house at a Music Hall:

'. . . nearly every evening the theatre is packed to suffocation; the admission is 1d. the gallery, 2d. the pit, 3d. and 6d. the upper circle and boxes. On the night of our visit there wasn't room to cram another boy in the place; the gallery and pit were full of boys and girls from eight to fifteen . . . and the bulk of the audience in the other parts were quite young people'.

Even so young an audience was not uncontrolled, although the methods adopted were primitive:

'Of course there are disturbances, but the remedy is short and effective. Two young gentlemen in the dress circle fought and used bad language to each other. Quick as lightning the official was upstairs with a solitary policeman, the delinquents were seized by the collar, and, before they could expostulate, flung down a flight of steps and hustled out into the street with a celerity that could only come from constant practice.' [*4*]

The practice was however undertaken by a solitary policeman, who patrolled the hall as did the policeman whom Macready employed patrol the rear of the Drury Lane auditorium in the 1840s, so disturbances cannot have been excessive.

That the audience in the halls was composed of young people is not surprising; working youths would find that the admission charges made light and warmth and entertainment theirs two or three evenings a week, whereas the regular theatres would of course have been impossibly dear for them. However, as they were so young, clearly some of the Victorians' anxiety about music hall audiences' supposed rowdiness and violence derives from their fear of city youth in general. There was a considerable body of unemployed and homeless youngsters within the city's 15,000 beggars—a group which also gave notable unease to the literate middle class. There was too, throughout the period from 1843 to 1880, increasing (and justified) anxiety over the high rates of other forms of delinquency—in 1847 for example the capital's Metropolitan Police took more than 62,000 people into custody; 16,000 were below the age of twenty, nearly 4,000 below the age of fifteen, and 362 below the age of ten. In the 1850s it was officially stated that there were in London a total of 30,000 lawless and deserted children.

Although there was in the 1870s and 1880s in particular a great philanthropic movement, which culminated in the formation of the Royal Society for the prevention of Cruelty to Children in 1884, it was education which was viewed as the proper antidote to youthful lawlessness. The *1870 Education Act* was seen, in the eyes of the literary establishment, as an act of control, and self-defence by the state. As one commentator said:

'The system is not a largesse to the recipient, but a natural measure of self-defence on the part of the government which educates. It is necessary, in a democratic form of government, that the voters should be so far educated as to be reasonably relieved from the danger of deception by interested parties.' [5]

The music hall owners were certainly seen as interested parties, enticing the young from their work, and giving low and gaudy notions to the defenceless populace under the guise of harmless pleasure. 'In the music hall', wrote J. Ewing Ritchie sadly in 1880, 'people go to be amused'. It was a period when there was not only a new and rigid distinction between 'art' and 'entertainment', but a period in which entertainment was, for many of the middle class, not merely void of improvement but positively sinful.

The word 'art', which was adopted by the West End managers until the first World War as a proper descriptive word for their business, underwent two important changes in the nineteenth century in its use. Until about 1840, it actually meant any creative activity; thereafter it began to acquire overtones of spirituality and unworldliness, so that when a young lady was described as 'artistic' it implied she was well above mundane practicalities. It then, particularly through the pervasive influence of Matthew Arnold, acquired an additional overtone of being educational and improving in its effect. By the 1890s anything which claimed to be 'art' was not claiming to be worthwhile because it was creative and enjoyable, but worthwhile because it was possessed of an etherial and mysterious quality, which was above the mundane and commonplace in itself, but mysteriously educated and improved commonplace folk who came into contact with it. An important effect of this sharp change in the meaning of the word was that the non-artistic was denigrated. Mere entertainment was seen as a different order of things from theatrical 'art', and, until the turn of the century, the songs of the music hall were not to be judged by the minds that took seriously the high drama of H. J. Byron and Robertson and Jerrold. The West End theatre, particularly under the dominance of Irving, was 'art', and was not averse to calling itself a school of learning and improvement, and generally placing itself upon the side of the angels. An aspect of that was the way in which all the former faults of the vagabond player— fecklessness, immorality, illiteracy—were now passed off on to the entertainers, while the new West End was a part of the march 'onward and upward'.

There was considerable anger on behalf of some writers and the entertainment managers over this widening division within the theatre. In *Patience*, W. S. Gilbert's somewhat heavy-handed satire on the aesthetic movement, which was produced in 1881, the new notions of art are ponderously satirised:

Bunthorne Don't be frightened - it's only poetry.

Patience Well, if that's poetry, I don't like poetry.

Bunthorne (Eagerly) Don't you? (aside) Can I trust her? (Aloud) Patience, you don't like poetry - well, between you and me, **I** don't like poetry. It's hollow, unsubstantial, unsatisfactory. What's the use of yearning for Elysian Fields when you know you can't get 'em, and would only let 'em out on building leases if you had 'em? [6]

And the wish (as it seemed to the singers) to take the raffishness and spontaneity from theatre-going, was regularly mocked on the music halls themselves, notably in an Albert Chevalier song:

> *In the great good time, the goody good time,*
> *When Cardinals and Bishops go a-mumming.*
> *A magic lantern show will be considered very fast,*
> *Sing hey for the good time coming!*
> *And folks will say, 'How nice to have a moral show at last,'*
> *Sing hey for the good time coming!*
> *The Ballet, too, will be a real credit to our stage,*
> *Decorum and Propriety of course will be the rage,*
> *You'll never see a dancer under fifty years of age,*
> *In the very, very good time coming.*

The piece is interesting because it refers, once more, to the refined theatre's mistrust of youth. We tend to overlook the fact that in the 80s and 90s music hall performers were markedly younger than were the West End stars, just as their audiences were younger than those at the Lyceum and St. James's.

The entertainment managers were of course aware that theirs was indeed a different kind of management from that newly practised in the West End theatres. First, for the owners, the capital outlay was less. An ornate theatre such as Her Majesty's, with raked auditorium, tiered and curved galleries and with rich decoration, cost £50,000 when it was reconstructed in 1869. By contrast the Middlesex Music Hall cost £12,750 in 1878, and Moy's Music Hall (later the Victoria Palace) cost £12,000 in 1901; the straighter lines, flat floors for the tables and the simpler decoration all keeping down cost. Running costs too were very much lower. The larger houses employed only a skeletal stage staff, and the orchestra was smaller than in the sumptuous West End theatres. The popular areas were large—the gallery at the Middlesex held nearly half the audience—and it was not unusual to have two distinct 'houses' each evening. Without programmes to sell, cloakrooms to man, or bars to staff at some distance from the auditorium, the music halls were also cheaper and easier to run front of house. Overall, running costs were much lower, capital repayments or rentals much lower—and therefore the halls could succeed by attracting huge audiences at low admission charges, rather than a 'stalls' audience which would pay a high admission charge and then pay a considerable number of 'extras' to swell the receipt. Certainly the music halls were very profitable for their

66

managers: Henri Gros left £10,000, Adney Payne £20,000, Herbert Sprake of Collins Music Hall more than £50,000. [7]

The growing schism between artistic theatre and the theatre of popular entertainment much annoyed John Hollingshead, who, from its opening in 1868 was for 18 years the manager of the Gaiety in the Strand. For the Gaiety was placed by the London literati on the wrong side of the divide, as Hollingshead wryly recalls:

> 'What was the title of my theatre? 'The Gaiety.' This at once stamped it as a 'place of amusement'. I could embellish amusement as much as I liked. I could flavour occasionally with High Art Sauce, but though an old literary colleague of Charles Dickens, William Makepeace Thackeray and Dr. Norman Macleod, I had to steer clear of the rocks of literature, properly so-called.' [8]

From the first, he recalls, a theatre such as the Gaiety was seen by the West End establishment as being 'an almost impious attempt to widen the area of theatrical enterprise', and almost as soon as it did open it was labelled as being a 'place of amusement', the 'home of burlesque'.

In fact the programme at the Gaiety was extremely wide—only 8% of the 500 pieces given there during Hollingshead's management were burlesque—and the achievement was in finding a large audience at the same theatre for such a mixed programme. He presented ballet, new English drama, amateur and professional pantomime, concerts, opera and operettas such as Gilbert and Sullivan's version of *Trial by Jury*, to which he gave the first performance. There were in addition distinguished seasons of work by major European companies, in particular the notable season of the Comedie Francaise in 1879, when that company played their entire repertory in six weeks. In that period the theatre took £19,685.19s.6d. from 36 evening performances and 7 matinees, an average of £468.10s. per performance. The leading member of that company, Sarah Bernhardt, found the Gaiety audience notable for its 'attention, its kindness and its emotion'. She received, according to the *Gaulois* on 5th June 1879, 'an ovation . . . unique in the annals of the theatre in England'.

Such successes were however not sufficient to remove the taint of being primarily concerned with mere amusement. Hollingshead bitterly points out that the only failures, ironically, were when the Gaiety produced 'the old drama', which was supposed to contain the virtuous qualities which the popular theatre had neglected:

> 'The revival, if only for a few hours, of a class of play that had

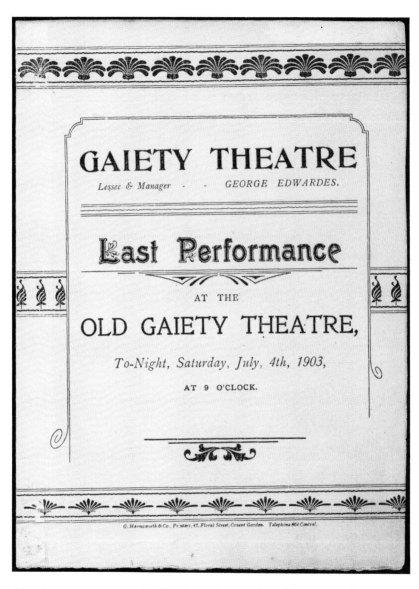

GAIETY THEATRE

Lessee & Manager - - GEORGE EDWARDES.

Last Performance

AT THE

OLD GAIETY THEATRE,

To-Night, Saturday, July, 4th, 1903,

AT 9 O'CLOCK.

G. Harmsworth & Co., Printers, 12, Floral Street, Covent Garden. Telephone 664 Central.

The free programme for the last night at the old Gaiety Theatre. Sir Henry Irving, appropriately enough, spoke its 'epitaph'.

degraded a fine race of actors and actresses, was a good object lesson for the many ladies and gentlemen who talked glibly about 'the decline of the drama'. [*9*]

His theatre of course was popular; it accommodated 2,000 people and in Hollingshead's 18 years of management it closed on average for only one week a year and presented 959 matinees. It could not be accused of entertaining rowdy audiences—after a brief period when it was 6d. the gallery admission was in fact raised again to 1/- because too boisterous a clientele was being attracted—but it was enough that it did not stay within the guidelines for 'art' which the West End coterie professed. Hollingshead saw that group as having a restrictive influence; it had become a profession 'more trade unionist, in the worst sense, than the Bar or the Church'. He had no regard for the 'old restrictive practices of management', but sought a free market, 'I not only believed in competition, I positively revelled in it'. Yet the categorisation of theatres as being either artistically refined or otherwise defeated him, and in the eyes of the London establishment it was impossible to have a situation in which burlesque competed with 'art':

> 'Whether burlesque is art, or art is burlesque, it is not necessary . . . to attempt to determine. Any theatre devoted to its performance is at once stamped as the 'house of call' for fools and idiots. Its stage is supposed to copy the vilest dens described in Pierce Egan's *Life in London*. That is a lie, of course, and there is not other word for it.' [*10*]

So extreme was the divide however that when he had the original notion of running the Victoria Tavern (the Old Vic) as a reformed music hall, he felt himself too tainted with mere 'entertainment' to be able to play a role in its administration. 'My connection with the Gaiety was not considered a good and safe qualification for me to take a leading part in carrying out my idea.'

The essential differences between what was now considered 'art' and what was considered 'entertainment' were clear enough, but most marked perhaps in the behaviour of their audiences. The West End audiences were most clearly defined by their elaborate dress, decorum and that ability to undertake 'the enjoyment of boredom in distinguished company'. Thus William Archer describes as West End audience behaving beautifully on the opening night of Irving's *Lear* in 1892:

> 'A very large—a much too large—portion of the text had been cut

away, and what remained of the part of Lear, one half at least was inaudible. Seated in the sixth row of the stalls, not far from the middle. I heard practically nothing of the mad scenes, and even in the earlier and later passages it was only by closely following the printed text that I could make out with any clearness what was going on. The audience in the pit and gallery, I am convinced, cannot have heard one-fifth part of Lear's words; and I know of no stronger testimony to Mr. Irving's prestige and personal magnetism that they sat still and silent and respectful throughout, uttering no syllable of protest.' [11]

Such a presentation, one would hazard, could not have been received with such docility had it been presented at an 'entertainment' house such as the Gaiety. There the audience was, as Mme. Bernhardt had noted, attentive, but it was not prepared to take injections of high theatrical art intravenously.

The clear distinction in social behaviour had also a powerful effect upon the managerial ambitions of Oswald Stoll and hence, indirectly, on the eventual fate of the music hall. Stoll was, with his partner Moss, the largest presenter of entertainment in the provinces. However when he sought to take a West End theatre in the nineties, not only was he refused but, more hurtfully, he was not allowed to join the Theatrical Managers' Association. So the two decided that, given the bullish state of the theatrical market, it was best to use some of their existing £1,500,000 capital to build new theatres in the West End area. Accordingly Moss built the Hippodrome (Later The Talk of the Town) and Stoll himself built the Coliseum—in which he presented a new form of variety, combining elements of 'straight' theatre, ballet, speciality acts and the more respectable music hall performers, with suitably mounted 'quality' presentations. The investment in the new theatre was high—the revolving stage alone cost £70,000 more than five times the entire cost of building the Middlesex Music Hall—and it seated 3,389. In essentials however it was a refined West End theatre, and not a music hall. There was no drinking in the auditorium, and the bars were small and mean for the size of auditorium. It was ornately decorated, and staffed with bewigged house 'flunkeys'. It employed a large orchestra, and had above their pit lushly furnished boxes. The original populist schedule, of presenting four shows a day, was soon abandoned, and the theatre ran in the evenings like other West End venues. Above all, the presentations were expensive, polished and without the raw

70

An example of Stoll's wide-ranging variety bills, in which ballet, serious 'legitimate' actors and music hall performers appeared together.

give and take between performers and audience that characterised other music halls. Thus 'entertainment' was re-dressed, made respectable, fitted into its ornate new home, and so entered the West End.

And, shortly afterwards, Stoll and Moss joined the Theatrical Managers' Association and were able to disdain the unrefined elements of popular entertainment. Both were on the General Committee which chose the bill for the first Royal Command Variety Performance at the Palace Theatre on 1st July 1912. Naturally the country's leading music hall entertainer, Marie Lloyd, was not invited to be on the bill, for she so obviously was an 'entertainer' of the common people.

6
The Tools of Management

Although the term 'middle class', referring to audiences, could not comprehend the same kind of people in both 1750 and 1880, it is roughly correct to say that in terms of class the theatre was in much the same relationship to its West End audience in 1750 as in 1880. The intervening period had seen the theatre pass, for the first time since the medieval period, under a rule that was essentially popular; it then passed out again into middle class control.

Professor Michael R. Booth

The tools of management available to theatre managers in the middle of the nineteenth century were primitive. Although control over expenditure, particularly in shared managements, was precarious—it is likely that a major cause of Mathews' bankruptcy was the uncontrolled extravagance of his wife and partner—it was the near-impossibility of controlling *income* that made anything more than the crudest long-term budget an impossibility. There were three major reasons for this. First, the terms on which a manager operated throughout the season were subject to constant variation; he did not know whether he would be forced to yield benefit nights for his players, for example, which could give large parts of the receipt for a popular production to a favourite player, and he did not always know whether the theatre owners would use their allocated seats in the theatre, or would sell them and further cut into the manager's likely income. Second, the systems of cash control within the theatres themselves were crude and unreliable; it was frequently the case that box keepers and other staff would be in the habit of giving 'orders' (free admission) to their friends, and, if they were dishonest, the ticketing systems allowed them fairly easily to extract money from the daily receipt before it was taken to the manager's office. Third, forecasting income was impossible, for there was no reliable advance booking system which would enable him to know what was the long-term demand for a production.

The manager lived in a state of constant tension, never knowing what kind of house he would have until the evening was well begun, and constantly having to change productions in order to try, by instinct, better to please the patrons. Thus when Macready noticed one night in 1840, playing *Macbeth*, that 'the half-price had fallen away', he decided to put up a production of *Othello* the following Monday! In such circumstances the actor managers in particular had little time to exercise any kind of daily supervision over the account books, and it was with a kind of weary resignation, later that same season, that Macready had a short meeting with his treasurer Robertson, and 'found myself about £2,200 to make up, to bring in even balance; profit is therefore beyond all hope'. [1]

Few managers had any kind of capital to fall back upon in a difficult period, and the other possibility, that of raising prices, was felt to be impossible as the memories of the Old Price riots in Covent Garden in 1809 (when an attempt had been made to raise prices) remained strong. Even when prices were raised a little in the late 60s provincial houses still yielded very little. 'These small towns are worth nothing', Phelps wrote to his wife from Bradford in 1869, 'Even with raising the prices, £35, or at the utmost £40, is a great house. On Saturday, at Huddersfield, we turned them away, and yet, with 4s. boxes, etc., it did not quite reach £40, and Friday the same'. London managers were also constrained by the rigid upper limit on income from a full house, although their figures were larger. Kean put the problem in context in a speech from the stage of the Princess's theatre in 1859, at the end of nearly a decade of successful management there:

'I may say that in this little theatre, where £200 is considered a large receipt, and £250 an extraordinary one, I expended in one season alone, a sum little short of £50,000.' [2]

Such a season was exceptional, for the financial summary of his management shows that he spent an average of £27,111 per season. Nevertheless his figures for large and extraordinary receipts are probably typical of the whole of his management in the 1850s. The maximum receipt, had every seat been sold, was £309, but the silver and gold 'tickets', the 'orders', the inevitable unreliability of some of the staff and the great difficulty of selling all, or most, seats regularly without the filtration of demand by a booking system, meant that between £200 and £250 represented very good business. The high expenditure for his lavish productions kept his account on an extraordinary knife edge; on average he made about £200 profit in each season, and on the management as a whole made a final profit of £2,000.

The other obvious variant was the number of performances given in a season. Custom too kept this remarkably static in the 1840s and 50s. Six performances a week were given through the 'season', which ended in early July; in general theatres tried not to close during the fit up and rehearsal of a new piece, so there were regular nightly performances, the plays or entertainments chosen for the next few days being 'given out' at the end of the evening in a stage announcement. There were early attempts to add matinee performances. In 1853 E. T. Smith presented a 'morning juvenile performance' at Drury Lane in January and presented a matinee performance of Brooke in *Othello* in September of the same year. Hollingshead presented regular matinees at the Gaiety theatre in 1871 onwards, and Marie Litton had regular matinee performances at the Imperial theatre in 1880. In general such performances were of course only accessible to the leisured classes. In view of their general managerial objectives it is not surprising therefore, that the Bancrofts introduced matinees into their own work at the Prince of Wales's in 1878. Rather more surprising is that following the *1871 Bank Holiday Act*, which gave the English six such free days, other theatres did not by and large present special bank holiday matinee performances. By the 1870s it *was* common to have matinees of pantomimes, but Hollingshead saw no reason why the practice could not have been widely extended in the theatre, except, as he says, that there was an agreement that competition between the central theatres should not become 'too intensive', and therefore 'the old restrictive practices of management' should be retained.

Many lessee-managers had however a greater flexibility over income than the rigidity of prices and the fixed regularity of performances might imply. One additional source from 1870 was in the income from theatre bars, and refreshment areas. There had been continuous complaint that it was not possible to have a good meal out in London from the 1840s to the 1860s, and the restaurant, said Charles Dickens Jr. 'as it has been for many years understood in Paris, practically had no

SYNOPSIS of TWENTIETH SEASON
ROYAL LYCEUM THEATRE.

Sole Lessee and Manager ... HENRY IRVING.

From Week ending Friday, the 27 July 1896   day of To 23 July 1897

RECEIPTS.

Date	Play	Nett.	Total

EXPENDITURE.

WORKING EXPENSES

HOUSE
Printing
Advertising
Bill Posting
STAGE—
Salaries
Supers
Stage Expenses
Gas
Lime-Light
Author's Fees
Orchestra
PRODUCTION ACCOUNT
CAPITAL ACCOUNT
EXPENDITURE ON HOUSE
LAW EXPENSES & AUDIT

Bram Stoker's synopsis of the twentieth season at the Royal Lyceum Theatre.

place in London.' By the 1870s however there were some thirty or forty restaurants open to families in central London, and the habit of combining dining 'out' with a theatre visit became an acceptable middle class ritual. Some new theatres built after 1865 had as much foyer and dining space as auditorium space in stalls and circle areas, as it was assumed that the better-off customers would, if not always eat, certainly make a habit of regularly drinking on the premises.

Arrangements over the refreshment areas were varied. At one extreme were the caterers Spiers and Pond, who built the Criterion restaurant in Piccadilly at a cost of £100,000 in 1873 and who owned the theatre contained within it (which they let on a weekly rental of £50 to its first manager, Mr. W. Duck). At the other were the managers who sublet their own restaurant or bars to professional caterers. Augustus Harris, when he entered upon management at Drury Lane in 1885, gained his initial working capital by subletting the bars for a year for £1,000. Between the two were a variety of arrangements. Sometimes owners 'reserved' the bars, so they were not a part of the lessee's concern, and occasionally managers ran them directly. By the 1880s it was not uncommon for the profit from the bars in a successful theatre to yield income as high as the theatre rental, and a major factor in the comfortable profits Harrison and Maude made at the Haymarket theatre between 1896 and 1905, was that they ran the bars, which were succinctly advertised as being 'Under Direct Control. Fuller's Sweets'.

From the 1860s theatre managers increasingly sought to make theatre-going a full social experience, and one which would yield to the management the full profits from a Victorian night out. As early as 1862 Boucicault opened the old Astley's, remodelled as the Theatre Royal, Westminster, in a fashion which promised in one respect to be like the National Theatre on the South Bank:

> 'He converted the old 'ring' into an elaborate arrangement of stalls and pit; the bygone Adelphi system of intermediate 'pit stalls' he also introduced. The immense size of the *salle* admitting of greater alterations, Mr Boucicault placed between the stalls proper and the orchestra a sort of miniature garden of shrubs, flowers and fountains, the effect of which in hot weather was extremely pleasant. Adjoining the theatre, and on the site of what was known as 'Astley's Cottage', Mr Boucicault had projected a vast *cafe*, which was to be constructed of iron and glass with foyers for promenaders between the acts, and an open-air

restaurant on the flat Moorish roof commanding a view of the river.' [3]

In 1868 Hollingshead opened the Gaiety, with a promise to his new audience:

'NOTE. — The Saloons will be opened on the same night (December 21, 1868) and will communicate with the theatre on every level. The expensive Cafe and Restaurant attached to the theatre will be opened in a few weeks.' [4]

Unlike Boucicault, Hollingshead built and opened his restaurant. Trade was so good that a decade later a new restaurant was built 'at immense cost' by Spiers and Pond, and opened in 1878. The leading feature of the New Gaiety Restaurant was that it communicated directly with the theatre. The newly-alert city authorities however demanded that this be changed, so that people passing from restaurant to theatre had technically to go 'outside', a piece of bureaucracy that infuriated Hollingshead.

From the 1880s there were few new attempts to place restaurants within the theatre building itself, but there were many things besides alcoholic drinks sold in bars and foyers. From the late 1870s coffee and ice cream were sold in the fashionable theatres in addition to the boxed chocolates which were popular with ladies' parties. In 1878 John Hare introduced 'the genteel traditions of the Prince of Wales's' to the Court theatre and ices and coffee were handed round the pit during the intervals.

Profit from the sale of refreshments, though important, was not as significant in the history of managerial control as the development of booking techniques. In the 1860s Covent Garden had some bookable numbered seats in stalls and boxes but there, as in all other London theatres, less fashionable areas were not bookable. Doors were opened a few minutes before the performance, and the customer bought at the entrance a metal medallion, which was taken from him at the entrance to pit or gallery. The manager's only means of checking whether he received the actual monies paid in admission was to check the receipt against the number of medallions taken at the door; plainly, if the box keeper and doorman were in league the manager had little chance. One notorious abuse was for the gallery doorkeeper to unscrew the knob at the top of the brass stair rail and to slide down a number of medallions to the box keeper, who would re-sell them and split the receipt from their first sale with his ally.

As booking for stalls, boxes and dress circle grew in the 1870s it proved equally liable to abuse by incompetent or dishonest staff. The leading West End theatres, in the 1870s, would send each day a certain number of blank card 'tickets' to the libraries (the commercial lending libraries that sold theatre tickets as a sideline) and instruct them as to the range of numbered seats they covered, leaving the librarians to fill in the date and the number of the seat by hand. Meanwhile, at the theatre's own box-office, tickets ordered by post or bought at the box-office window were also filled in by hand. When the monies, records of sales and unsold tickets were collected by messenger at the end of the day and returned to the theatre box-office for checking against in-house sales, it was, not unreasonably, common to discover discrepancies. These difficulties grew as theatres tried advance booking, still trusting to the clerks in the libraries and box-office to fill in the correct date for upwards of seven performances ahead. There were duplications, wrong dates, and times when the record of sales (for which purpose the stub is nowadays kept in the printed ticket book) did not tally with what was written upon the card 'ticket'. Hawtrey was told that 'doubles were common' by his staff, and Leverton recounts the story of a sacked box-office manager who, undetected, confused a theatre's advance booking out of pique. [5]

The first major step towards a more controlled system was taken by Hawtrey in 1884, when dealing with the great demand for tickets for *The Private Secretary*. He suspected he was being cheated and the box-office keeper had 'Left to find employment elsewhere':

> 'Now though I had every confidence in my business-manager's honesty, I decided to look into the matter. My brother John told me that during the last month he had investigated, as far as he could, every double that had taken place and had come to the conclusion that there was something radically wrong with the methods in force. Evidently there was no supervision over the box-office!'

A Mr Evans, from the firm of Smallfield and Rawlings, was engaged to establish a system of check and counter check over all the theatre accounts and give a monthly statement to the management. Within two days Evans, a chartered accountant, had detected collusion between the box-office staff to defraud Hawtrey. The clerk involved with the late box-office keeper was sacked also. Hawtrey and Evans devised a system which was then quite new:

> 'We provided a separate bound book of tickets and counterfoils

Theatre tickets before Hawtrey's introduction of the 'numbered book'. The seat number was written in by hand.

80

for each night, with the date, number of seat, part of the house and price printed on each ticket, doing away altogether with date writing, and making it impossible for the box-office keeper to sell tickets for the same seats twice, as there would be only one in existence for each seat.' [6]

Although expensive at first, the printing of theatre tickets was taken up as a commercial proposition, and soon the system was in widespread use. George Edwardes told Hawtrey it was 'the best check on the box-office ever invented'. It became possible to book further ahead in long runs—*The Private Secretary* ran for 784 performances—and plans of theatre seating were more readily displayed. In 1887 Hays published his *Plans for the Principal Theatres in London.* By 1890 Stoker was able to book *Ravenswood* six weeks ahead at the Lyceum, and even that did not exhaust immediate demand; Stoker adds 'I may say we were *booked* that long, for as each day's advance sheet was opened it became quickly filled'.

The new system did not merely give better control to theatre managements, it also made theatre-going more difficult for the working class. Box-offices and libraries were of course largely set within the area now known as West End, and open for advance booking during the day from 10 a.m. According to the Haymarket box-office manager Leverton, there was a steady stream of bookers until one o'clock, and then demand fell away. Working class people could not easily book at such times and because of that, and other obvious reasons, were not a part of the audience in the bookable sections. For the wrong class the 'libraries' were in any case forbidding:

'Some of them had their own idiosyncrasies, which had to be studied. For example, one of the leading ticket agents is Lacon and Ollier's, near Bond Street . . . the head of the firm was a stately old gentleman called Charles Ollier. Lacon's had a very distinguished clientele, and Charles Ollier would not sell or allow to be sold in his office any other seats than the highest priced ones—orchestra stalls or private boxes. If a stranger entered, and dared to ask for dress circle or—worse still—upper circle tickets, the venerable Mr Ollier would lead him courteously to the door, hold it wide open for his exit, and say, with infinite suavity:

'You will be able to buy *that* class of ticket opposite, at Messrs Blanks.'

And the delicate emphasis with which he stressed the words

'*that* class of ticket' would reduce the vulgar stranger to perspiring shame'. [7]

There was also some feeling amongst the regulars that the new printed tickets were insufficiently stylish for the important West End audience. Oscar Wilde complained to Tree at the Haymarket that he got 'a nicer ticket' on a penny railway ride and insisted that a special one be drawn up for him on card. In the 1890s the St. James's theatre indeed reverted to printing tickets on stiff card, of the same size as invitations to other fashionable social gatherings.

The social rituals of booking were thus made increasingly attractive to London's leisured classes, and proportionately forbidding to the working class. The box-office managers who had been, in the 1850s, frequently described as 'rough and unshaven' now wore morning coats and, as Leverton describes, went home in the late afternoon in order to change into evening dress, which they, like the house attendants, habitually wore. The cost to the audience of dressing for the theatre was not inconsiderable, but the associated manners and conversation were as daunting for the uninitiated. The box-office managers' names were given in the advertisements in favoured newspapers, so regular customers were encouraged to have the same kind of social relationship with them as with an established departmental head at Harrods, Swan and Edgar or the Army and Navy stores. Theatre staff knew the regulars personally, and for outsiders the sense of closed privilege around those who were able to book regularly for the West End theatre must have been strong.

The narrowing of focus in the booking rituals was accompanied by a similar narrowing in advertising; as management tools became sharper they focussed increasingly upon the well-to-do in their whole marketing strategy. After 1843 advertising had been by bills and street displays—the sandwich board was a favoured method—linked with discreet notices in the London newspapers announcing the opening of a new piece. This was on occasion accompanied by some discreet copy, although in general newspaper puffs in the mid-nineteenth century seem less luxuriant than those described in Sheridan's *The Critic* as being all the rage in eighteenth century London. When, in the late forties, shops more commonly had plate glass windows the hanging bill became more popular, and as Priscilla Metcalf says, the vast improvement schemes in central London were a perfect opportunity for the bill sticker:

'The Advertising Man was coming into his own. The many hoardings put up around new building sites and street improvements were a field for bill stickers. Some of their favourite spots, beside the hoarding around Trafalgar Square until late April 1844, and then around Nelson's pedestal for years, included the fence at the top of the stairs leading to the steamboat station at the North End of Waterloo Bridge, houses about to come down for the extension of Cranbourn Street, and the West side of St. James's Street where the Conservative Club was going up— hoardings postered in aid of Guinness's Dublin stout or So and So's Gout and Rheumatic Oil, not to mention the playbills.' [8]

By 1862 Webster, defending himself against an action before the Queen's Bench, said that for theatre managers there were four kinds of advertisements. They were 1) advertisements in newspapers, 2) placarded posters, 3) shop bills, and 4) the playbill used within the theatres themselves. In the same decade the practice grew of having permanent painted wall advertisements for a theatre, and of taking space on the omnibus and cab panels for general notices about the theatre, or a long-running show.

The removal of the stamp duty on newspapers in 1855 signalled the start of the great newspaper expansion, but it was not until the advent of what Matthew Arnold called 'the new Journalism' in the 1880s that newspaper advertising became for theatre managers a pre-eminent medium of contact with their target audiences. The coming of *The Star* (1888), *The Sun* (1893) and the *Daily Mail* were not important because theatre managers advertised in them (some never did) but because they divided the reading public by class and interests accurately enough for the managers to be sure that in advertising in the serious papers they would not, as with bill posting and street advertising, be scattering their message indiscriminately throughout London's population. They would, if they advertised in *The Times* and *The Telegraph*, be reaching with great precision the well-to-do and literate, and it was those newspapers which spearheaded the advertising campaign. *The Telegraph* indeed ran a daily feature called 'Under The Clock' which spread the casts of all West End productions around a circle, like the numbers on a clock face—representing to provincial actors no doubt something of a charmed circle of privilege. In working class sheets such as *Tit Bits* and *The Police Gazette* no West End advertising appeared.

The old playbill was replaced by programmes in most West End theatres by the mid-1880s. At first these were printed by the catering firms, and were three-sided, selling for 6d. in the well-to-do houses. Irving introduced a daily programme at the Lyceum in 1880, and in the following years a number of elaborate programmes made their appearance. In some theatres—such as the Haymarket from 1886-96—there were cardboard programmes for the stalls and thinner paper ones for less genteel parts. However all theatre programmes soon had two uses other than simply informing the audience of the scenes and the actors' names. First, advertising space was sold on them, so that in addition to the 6d. purchasing price they represented a valuable source of extra income—and secondly they were plainly designed to be taken back and displayed in the home, and were thus a potential source of image-building and further advertising. The advertisements are generally indicative of the class of clientele, and no attempt was made to hide the fact that they reached 'the superior class of the buying public'. The design was tasteful enough for the programme to be displayed on an occasional table at home in order to stimulate further conversation about the theatre; the Savoy, for example, offered in the 1880s a 6d. programme which was printed on card and included on a gilt-edged cover coloured sketches of the Gilbert and Sullivan characters.

Thus the managers gradually gained control of the management systems, and by the end of the century could budget realistically, control their cash flow through advance booking and more disciplined internal systems, and could adjust demand rather better by the more sophisticated advertising means at their disposal. But each stage in gaining greater control involved less concern with the generality of the public, and more upon the favoured middle class. That concentrated wooing had two awkward results. First was the fact that it often became more important to indulge in the social rituals the favoured classes demanded than to work on the plays. As J. H. Barnes complained in 1908:

> 'In recent years I have rehearsed in a theatre all day—and sometimes nearly all night—where the manager and leading actor would be called away from rehearsal almost every hour to attend to social matters, or meet private friends.' [9]

Second was the fact that within the auditoriums there was increasing concentration upon 'serving' the richer elements, who could be persuaded to buy food, drinks, expensive programmes and other souvenirs, and thus provided an ever-increasing percentage of the

84

income of the theatre. This explains why, in the theatres built around the turn of the century, there was such a difference between the space, comfort and services provided for the richer, booked, parts of the house, and those provided for the 'popular' sections.

Indeed, even a manager such as Beerbohm Tree, who was considered to be something of a populist, proposed to actually *close* his gallery at Her Majesty's Theatre after opening his new theatre in 1897. It seemed to him to yield little in the way of income or benefit. He was dissuaded only by a tirade from G. B. Shaw:

'This gallery will not, I understand, be always used; but it seems to me it would be better, instead of wasting it on ordinary occasions, to set it apart at a charge of sixpence or even less for such faithful supporters of high art as the working man with a taste for serious drama—especially Shakespeare—and the impecunious student, male and female, who will go to the stalls and balcony later in life . . . For the working-man connoisseurs, though they represent a very small percentage of their class, yet belong to an enormously large class, and so are absolutely more numerous than might be expected from their relative scarcity.' [10]

Shaw's comments have an ironic ring, in view of the cinema's later capture of that 'enormously large class' which was so pointedly shunned by the West End theatre. Tree agreed to keep it open with some reluctance, aware that his theatre was so organised that it depended, like other West End venues, disproportionately upon the favours of the well-to-do. His stalls, for example, although occupying only 37% of the theatre's total capacity, yielded nearly 60% of box-office receipts.

Henry Irving, sketched by Phil May after dinner at the home of Sir Francis C. Burnand. Irving's appetite for high social living - which he bequeathed to West End managers in our own century - was prodigious.

7
Henry Irving and the Art of Conspicuous Consumption

He understood nothing of jobbery or finance. Sums of money were to him only counters in a game, to be used for the buying of everything possible with which to adorn his beautiful mistress, the Drama.

Ellaline Terriss, By Herself 1928

Although each generation of West End managers bewailed in public the huge and 'necessary' costs of theatre management, to claim that the cost of presenting plays in London *inevitably* rose after 1870, because of the preordained nature of the higher drama, is to stretch credulity. Plays cost more to present to the public because the managements arranged it like that. They employed more people than were necessary, vaunted a conspicuous extravagance as a means of establishing themselves as persons of the highest rank and, faced with the obvious inadequacies of their financial management, took refuge in blaming uncontrolled expenditure and poor forecasts of income upon some dark tradition of the theatre. It will not suffice to say that 'the public taste' demanded new extravagance in all things theatrical, as Bancroft and Irving were establishing themselves. Rather the public responded, as ever, to various forms of drama—Bancroft's refined realism and Irving's spectacular epics among them. But they responded equally to something as relatively spartan and inexpensive as Dickens' solo readings. The *Illustrated London News* described Dickens' performance at the [large] St. Martin's Hall in 1858, to what was described as 'a numerous audience':

'Without any aid from costume, or any extravagance of motion, by the mere power of facial expression, he impersonates the different characters of his stories, and brings them ideally, but vividly, before the spectator's mind. Mr. Dickens has invented a new medium for amusing an English audience, and merits the gratitude of an intelligent audience.' [1]

Interestingly, it *was* also within the power of the greatest spendthrift among the London managers, Henry Irving, to hold an audience without expensive settings and hordes of supporting players. The first time he had dinner with the man who was to be his lifelong manager, Bram Stoker, Irving 'stood up to recite a poem with which we had all been familiar from our schooldays, which most if not all of us had ourselves recited at some time', *The Dream of Eugene Aram*, and 'such was Irving's commanding force, so great was the magnetism of his genius, so profound was the sense of his dominance' that Stoker and his fellow diners sat spellbound. [2]

Irving's sense of dominance during his management at the Lyceum from 1879 to 1899 led him however in a different direction. He created a series of sumptuous and meticulously worked productions, and invested his tenure of the theatre with an extraordinary aura of priestly opulence. In Figure 4 a summary is given of the Lyceum expenditure 1879-1899. Obviously Irving worked to larger figures than had ever before appeared in theatre budgets. Stoker's final summaries [3] (for the Lyceum seasons only, excluding the figures for provincial and overseas tours) show that expenditure of £882,000 was however still more than matched by total receipts of £1,034,000. Irving's lowest expenditure on any new production in the repertoire, £1,100 on *Hamlet* in 1878, was as high as Phelps' highest, on *Pericles*. When he was established production costs soared, £15,402 on *Faust* in 1885, and £16,543 on *Henry VIII* in 1892. [4]

The stage expenses were of course particularly high, totalling some £628,000, or 71% of the total operating costs. Amongst those expenses the total salary bill is, considering that Irving himself took a salary of only £70 a week throughout his management, high. It was achieved by employing large numbers of actors to perform the style of production he favoured, rather than by paying most actors particularly well, unlike the Bancrofts' practice at the Haymarket. Younger players were paid between £5 and £10 a week, more established ones rose to £30 and £40, and some to £80. Ellen Terry was paid more, particularly for the U.S. tours, but Stoker is reticent about giving the precise figure. The vast size of the stage *corps* is further indicated by the expenditure on supernumeraries. When Irving began management he paid 6d. a night,

Figure 4

Summary of Expenditure at the Lyceum 1879-1899

Stage Expenses	£
Salaries	280,000
Supers	16,000
Stage Staff and Expenses	100,000
Lighting (Gas, Electric and Limelight)	32,000
Orchestra	47,000
Production costs	153,000
Front of House	
General Staff of Theatre	30,000
Expenses of working	56,000
Sundries	12,000
Other Categories	
Law and Audit	3,000
Insurance	7,000
Upkeep of the House	48,000
Other Working Expenses	
Printing	13,000
Newspaper Advertising	57,000
Bill-posting	15,000
Purchase of Plays and other fees	13,000
Total Expenditure	882,000

then 1/-, and finally 1/6. The total expenditure shows that, if a shilling were the average wage, the management paid for 320,000 super/nights during the management, an incredible *average* of 60 supers at each single performance at the Lyceum.

The Bancrofts had been the first London management to pay to dress their actors, no longer requiring them to bring their own costumes for a part. Of course that was for small cast plays. In productions such as *Faust*, the Irving management dressed more than 100 performers, contributing to astronomical production costs. It has subsequently invariably been the case that West End performers are dressed by the management; acting is thus one of the few activities in which professionals are not sometimes expected to wear their own clothes. Stories abound in each decade of conspicuous waste, ranging through C. B. Cochran's habit of scrapping whole sets of costumes at dress rehearsal to Hugh 'Binkie' Beaumont in 1934 getting rid of all the clothes Molyneux had designed, at a dress rehearsal, replacing them, *and* paying Molyneux a settlement. [5]

The new admiration for archeological accuracy in setting, and realistic detail in costumes and properties was not of course of itself to be deplored. What was to be questioned was whether the huge fees paid to the members of the Royal Academy who painted for Irving, and the expensive and much publicised search for exactly the right property, did not often have far more social effect off-stage than artistic effect on it. For the Royal Academicians had achieved in Victorian society precisely that rank to which the leading West End managers aspired. They were knighted—Alma-Tameda, who designed *Corialanus*, was *Sir Laurence*—and they mixed with Royalty, scholars and the fashionable bohemians as equals, one reason why Irving was liberal in his hospitality and payments to Alma-Tameda, Sir Edward Burne-Jones, Bart., Edwin Abbey R.A., Onslow Ford R.A., as well as to his regular designer, Hawes Craven[6]. By such patronage and, eventually, by meeting with them as an equal, he eased the passage of the West End elite into the privileged ranks of Victorian bohemia.

The costs for hospitality, not listed as a separate item by Stoker, were undoubtedly extremely high. Like much else they were not necessary, in the sense that they directly contributed to the play, but the late night suppers and receptions were important, then as afterwards, to achieve the ultimate aim of gaining and holding a position in the London social establishment, an aim towards which the play itself contributed only a part. Irving revived the old Beefsteak Club, in lavish rooms at the rear of the Lyceum, out of which during performances, according to John Martin Harvey, would drift the tantilising aroma of the midnight meal cooking for Irving and his guests. This seems to have been almost a nightly occurence, and Stoker, who of course knew the ultimate costs, remarks blandly that 'The ordinary hospitalities of the Beefsteak Room were endless'. However, even that room was insufficient for the grander gesture:

90

Henry Irving as Robespierre. As Ellen Terry commented 'A one-man piece. Henry, and over 250 supers'.

91

'Sometimes the Beefsteak Room, which could only seat at most thirty six people, was too small; and at such times we migrated to the stage. These occasions were interesting, sometimes even in detail. On the hundredth night of *The Merchant of Venice*, 14th February 1880, there was a supper party for three hundred and fifty guests. On 25th March 1882, ninety-two guests sat down to supper to celebrate the hundredth night of *Romeo and Juliet.*'

Such gatherings were extraordinarily lavish. At the 1880 one for example, the stage was transformed into a great scarlet and white pavilion. An unseen orchestra played in the wings, and when Irving gave the Royal Toast an unseen choir sang the national anthem. Meanwhile all the guests had a sumptuous five course meal washed down by Heidsieck 1874. Expenditure was probably greater for the reception given at Victoria's Jubilee in 1887, and again for the Diamond Jubilee of 1897. It is likely that more than 5,000 people were entertained at the Lyceum during the 20 years of Irving's management, and costs of such entertaining would certainly account for the majority of the £12,000 which appears in Stoker's summary as 'Sundries'.

Lavish expenditure on hospitality, particularly food and drink for the exclusive cafe society of the theatre, has continued to be a feature of West End 'production costs' since Irving, and little meetings at the Ivy restaurant, at the Savoy Grill, or at 'The Flat' (As Ivor Novello's West End rooms were known to intimates) thread through accounts of the theatre more densely even than accounts of eating and drinking in musical or literary reminiscences. It is hard to find any memories of the West End theatre written since Irving which do not prominently feature expensive dining habits. Reminiscence of that 'necessary' expenditure is always glorified as chic; darling Noel Coward suggesting 'one more little drink', brilliant Somerset Maugham showing 'august asperity' when Peter Daubeny crassly mixed a Martini badly for him[7], Henry Sherek tolerantly putting T. S. Eliot's unease at joining him for drinks and a meal down to the author's inexperience with worldly theatrical producers[8]. The tradition of The Beefsteak has lived on, albeit less robustly, for almost a century.

Of all 'necessary' production costs however, it is the £100,000 for 'Stage Staff and Expenses' which bears the closest scrutiny. For it was in the last years of the century that such costs escalated, at precisely the time when in other industries a new technological phase was cutting expenses in production. Did a generation that could both mass-produce and where necessary custom-build the exquisitely tooled machinery of the railways have to make changing scenery so cumbersome and so labour intensive as it was? Did the bills for gas lighting have to go on rising even though the cost of gas in London gradually came down? There was in some quarters more than a suspicion that the stage in London was already inefficient and overmanned. Dion Boucicault had written in 1862:

'In 1859 I built in New York the Winter Garden Theatre, capable of containing 2,500 persons, being very little less than the capacity of the Theatre Royal, Drury Lane. With the same entertainments as at the Adelphi Theatre, the Winter Garden consumed 20,000 feet of gas per week; the Adelphi consumes 100,000. The number of carpenters required to work the stage in London varies from 20 to 30; in New York the same work is done by six. Here we employ five or six gasmen; there the same work is performed by a man and a boy. While in management at the Adelphi theatre I saw three men endeavouring to move a piece of scenery; I caused a simple contrivance to be attached to it, and a child was then able to move it readily with his forefinger. One might suppose that such an economy of labour would have been generally adopted, but our English nature is suspicious of improvement and jealous of reform.' [9]

Stoker, who was proud of the efficiency and tight control of the managerial office of the Lyceum, found that the established 'rights' and 'customs' of the stage crew, with their rigid demarcation lines, utterly defeated efforts at change:

'There is the Master Machinist—commonly called Master Carpenter—the Property Master, the Gas Engineer, the Electric Engineer, the Limelight Master. In certain ways the work of these departments impinge on each other in a way to puzzle an outsider. Thus, when a stage has to be covered it is the work of one set of men or the other, but not of both. Anything in the nature of a painted cloth, such as tassellated flooring, is scenery, and therefore the work of the carpenters but a carpet is a 'property', and as such to be laid down by the property staff. A gas light or an electric light is to be arranged by the engineer of that cult, whilst an oil lamp or candle belongs to properties. The traditional laws which govern these things are deep seated in trade rights and customs, and are grave matters to interfere with.' [10]

Thus, well before 1900, the London theatre was divided into competing power blocs of management and technicians. Actors and writers were less organised, but managers and their stage crews were drawn up into the familiar twentieth century battle lines before unionisation brought such division to many technically advanced industries.

In the twentieth century it has sometimes been the case that theatre managers have blamed the problems of inefficiency, overmanning and overspending upon the unions. This will scarcely hold water. The Actors' Association, the ill-organised predecessor of the Actor's union, Equity, was never strong enough to insist upon extra manning, and it was not until 1922 that it made a serious attempt to create a 'closed shop', ensuring that theatres and production companies employed only professional actors. Even when Equity was formed, in 1930, it concerned itself only with the gradual establishment of *minimum* West End salaries—pittances in comparison with the huge sums managers had for years chosen to pay their favoured performers. The same point can be made about the musicians; patterns of manning and expenditure, wasteful and otherwise, were established in the West End long before the foundation of the Musicians' Union in 1931.

The truth is that the managers chose to pay actors and musicians in the West End increasingly well, in the last years of the nineteenth century, because high fees for professional artistes were an integral part of the new rank of the theatrical art. Thus the managers connived at inefficiency. And when, in 1935, the London Theatre Council was set up to 'secure the largest possible measure of co-operation between Managers and Artists for the safeguarding and development of the theatre as a part of the national life' its 20 members 'generally representative of Managers and Artists engaged in the production of plays' in the West End continued to create contracts which gave West End 'stars' salaries grossly disproportionate to those of actors in provincial repertory or in suburban theatres.

The case of the stage crew was however different. Their high wages were established by traditional rights and customs, rather than by the more recent aspirations of the managers. Thus at the Lyceum stage hands worked an eight hour day and were then paid overtime. The next four hours counted as a second 'day', and the following two hours as a third. As Irving would sometimes have three long rehearsals together, the stage crew could at such times by working for fourteen hours on three successive days, double their basic weekly wage. [11]

Unlike actors however stage crew developed an ability to threaten collective action, and their traditional rights and their willingness to act in industrial solidarity has given them a strange hold over much stage practice—a stranglehold so powerful it sometimes leads producers and actors to speak with strange obsequiance of their powers:

> 'At the end of last night's London premiere of *Antigone*, Sir Laurence Olivier made a curtain speech of some length in which he praised all the back room boys, including of course the electricians, who had worked so hard and against so many difficulties to make the production a success.
>
> This was rather puzzling as there is only one set, and most of the play consists of a duologue between Miss Vivien Leigh and Mr. George Relph.
>
> It is true that a clock chimes now and then, and always at the right moment, but I have known that to happen even in amateur productions.' [12]

Thus Beverley Baxter, writing of a production at the St. James's theatre, in 1949.

Favoured writers came also to be paid excessively by the managers, and in their turn to exercise some power. At the beginning of our period writers had to struggle to gain adequate recompense for their efforts. Before the *1833 Copyright Act*, and the *1842 Literary Copyright Act*, which plugged some of the holes left by the earlier legislation, an author had indeed no legal right in a dramatic presentation, and usually scripts were simply bought outright by managers, and then used as they wished[13]. However successful authors made arrangements with theatre managers of a more sophisticated kind, notably Boucicault who arranged with the manager Webster that he would take a regular part of the net profits during the whole of the run of *The Colleen Bawn* at the Adelphi[14]. In the sixties Robertson was taking a fixed £1 per performance of his plays from the Bancrofts; a sum which had risen to £10 a performance by the time of the Haymarket management. When Irving commenced management it had become common to both pay a fee for the rights of production, and a subsequent royalty during performance, and writers and managers combined both to rapidly increase and to publicise this new facet of the theatre's growing significance and prosperity. Gilbert and Sullivan made a well-publicised

£10,000 a year. Wilde made £7,000 in royalties from *Lady Windermere's Fan* alone. Henry James contemptuously rejected Alexander's offer of a payment of £2,000 for the rights of *Guy Domville*, evidently feeling that such a paltry sum insufficiently flattered the rank of either party.

Mention of the purchase of 'rights' in a play brings us to a final major extravagance of West End managers, once more inaugurated by Irving. This might be called pre-emptive expenditure, the costly buying out of a rival's ability to produce a success. First, it may take the form of keeping a talented performer under contract so that a rival may not have the use of those talents. In Irving's case it meant keeping young performers on the pay roll but giving them nothing challenging to play— Martin Harvey complains strongly, for example, about being treated by Irving in this way. It is a practice which has long continued, and even after the second World War rival managements were complaining that Tennent Plays Limited was doing just that with West End 'stars'. Second, it may take the form of buying up playscripts which are never used, but which a rival may not use either. Irving paid fees for, or bought options on, 27 plays which he did not produce; the average cost for each was £400, and thus during his management he spent £10,800 on work which presumably had merit but which was not to be shown in London[15]. Third—a practice which has grown in our own century—a rival may be pre-empted by being refused a theatre in which to house a promising production, and the theatre may be kept 'dark' or an unprofitable show maintained for a period until a new production is ready in which the owners have a more direct interest.

None of the expenditures we have discussed in this chapter can be called necessary in the sense in which the production expenses for a mystery play or an Elizabethan production were necessary. They do not arise from the demands of the art itself, but from the social rituals surrounding it.

The money may therefore be said to have been spent, not on the dramatic art, but on the social rituals appropriate to a new rank (for that segment of the theatrical profession which aspired to the new refinement). That was the significance of Irving's knighthood. Other theatre managers and other popular authors and composers had been knighted before Irving—Augustus Harris in 1891, Arthur Sullivan in 1883, for example—but Irving's knighthood was a benediction upon the art of the West End, as against the art of the older popular theatre. His entry into the highest rank was a watershed. The list of honours given thereafter to people with strong West End associations between 1895 and 1982 is impressive:

Sir Squire Bancroft	1897
Sir Charles Wyndham	1897
Sir Frances Burnand	1902
Sir John Hare	1907
Sir Arthur Wing Pinero	1909
Sir Beerbohm Tree	1909
Sir George Alexander	1911
Sir Johnston Forbes Robertson	1913
Dame May Whitty	1918
Dame Genevieve Ward	1921
Sir John Martin Harvey	1921
Sir Gerald Du Maurier	1922
Sir Charles Hawtrey	1922
Dame Ellen Terry	1925
Dame Madge Kendal	1926
Sir Nigel Playfair	1928
Sir John Gatti	1929
Dame Sybil Thorndike	1931
Sir Seymour Hicks	1935
Dame Marie Tempest	1937
Dame Irene Vanbrugh	1941
Dame Lilian Braithwaite	1943
Sir Lewis Casson	1945
Dame Edith Evans	1946
Sir Laurence Olivier	1947
Sir Ralph Richardson	1947
Sir Bronson Albery	1949
Sir Godfrey Tearle	1951
Sir John Gielgud	1953
Sir Cedric Hardwicke	1954
Dame Peggy Ashcroft	1956
Sir Alec Guinness	1959
Sir Michael Redgrave	1959
Dame Flora Robson	1960
Sir John Clements	1968
Sir Bernard Miles	1969
Sir Noel Coward	1969
Sir Emile Littler	1974
Sir John Mills	1976
Sir Peter Saunders	1982

97

By contrast folk primarily concerned with entertainment who have been honoured are comparatively few—Sir Edward Moss (1901), Sir Oswald Stoll (1919) and Sir George Robey (1954) among them. Equally short is any list of those honoured for their contribution to non-West End theatre; indeed such a list would probably contain only Sir Frank Benson (1916), Sir Ben Greet (1928), Sir Barry Jackson (1925) and Sir Donald Wolfit (1952). From the time of Irving's knighthood the higher echelons of the West End establishment yielded almost all candidates for high theatrical honours.

8
The West End 1890-1914

It is true that in the theatrical profession people are always talking Machiavelli, so to speak, and devising imaginary diplomacies and boycotts and compacts and the deuce knows what not; but at the first whiff of a success all that is flung to the winds.

Bernard Shaw, Advice to a Young Critic   1896

Between 1890 and 1914 the term 'West End' became a synonym for high sophistication and expense, a term which could be used by advertisers to sell fashionable clothes, luxury make-up, perfumes and entertainment equally. Horace Wyndham, who published his 'authorative work' on the social life in Mayfair during this period, mixed theatres with dance clubs, cabaret clubs, dining clubs and night clubs as being all a part of 'Bohemia, banquets, barmaids and other delights'[*1*]. For the middle classes London prospered; income tax was little more than a shilling in the pound, trade was booming, and overseas investments brought the country an unearned income of several hundred million pounds a year. Fortunes were as easily made in the theatre as elsewhere. Wilson Barrett, for example, went bankrupt in 1890, owing £40,000, but, after the huge success of his epic, *The Sign of the Cross*, he not only paid off all his debts in the period, but when he died in 1904 was worth £30,000.

The majority of Londoners however lived still in near-poverty. As C. H. Rolph rightly points out, although the 'average working wage' for 1900 is usually given as £1.15s, cookery books for the working class generally assume that *families* lived on about £1.10s. a week [*2*]— of which something like a quarter would go to pay the rent. In his autobiography Charlie Chaplin gives a poignant reminder that failure could, for theatre folk as much as anyone, mean near-starvation. His parents, both performers on the halls, had jointly earned some £65 a week. However, shortly after he was born, his parents separated, and his father then sent only 10s. a week in maintenance, a drop in income compounded by his mother losing her voice and her livelihood on the stage. Then 'from three comfortable rooms we moved into two, then into one, our belongings dwindling and the neighbourhoods into which we moved growing progressively drabber'. Eventually, there was no alternative, 'she was burdened with two children, and in poor health; and so she decided that the three of us should enter the Lambeth workhouse'. Two months later, their mother was able to take him and his brother Sydney out into London for the day:

'It was early morning and we had nowhere to go, so we walked to Kennington Park, which was about a mile away. Sydney had ninepence tied up in a handkerchief, so we bought half a pound of black cherries and spent the morning in Kennington Park, sitting on a bench eating them. Sydney crumpled a sheet of newspaper and wrapped some string around it and for a while the three of us played catch-ball. At noon we went to a coffee-shop and spent the rest of our money on a twopenny tea-cake, a penny bloater and two halfpenny cups of tea, which we shared between us!' [3]

Of course even a worker in stable employment earning £1.15s. a week could not afford the pleasures of the middle classes after he had paid rent upon a room. A good seat in a West End theatre cost between 5s. and 10s.6d., and an evening out in the West End therefore for two would easily have cost the entire £1.15s.

The leading West End manager was now a secure man of substance. W. Macqueen-Pope, whose theatre histories may be said not so much to analyse West End attitudes as to embody them, conveys something of the security of the manager:

'He was exclusively West End; he was not seen about all over the place. His was the dignity of distance and aloofness—you had to pay to see him and that gave him much value. And if perchance you happened to be in the West End—which really was the West End then—and came upon him face to face in Piccadilly, Pall Mall or Bond Street, or perhaps crossing Leicester Square en route for the Green Room club or the more cloistral calm of the Garrick Club, you would have raised your hat to him as a personality of eminence worthy of salute, and you would have been met with a similar courtesy on his part.' [4]

The male clubs do indeed play a central part in West End theatrical life from the 1890s to the present day, acting both as regular unofficial meeting houses for the theatrical establishment, and as institutions which impart their own ethical tone to business transactions between members. Their presence helps to explain the virtual exclusion of women from most West End management, although a secondary factor is the strong growth of Masonry in the West End theatre cabals around the turn of the century[5]. So even before the West End managers officially created their own organisation there was in effect an exclusive self-perpetuating caucus of people who considered themselves 'West End' and who resisted attempts by suburbanites, provincials and would-be innovators to enter their circles. The London stage, in David Holloway's words, 'was almost a closed corporation. There were two hundred members of the Green Room club, and it was from their number that all, or nearly all, the male members of West End casts, other than very small parts, were chosen.' [6]

There was increasing stability on the other side of the footlights, as a large audience settled comfortably into the theatre-going habits managements perpetuated as properly 'refined'. The old eighteenth century habit of subscription selling (a means of selling a season's seats to a known audience, saving trouble on both sides, and ensuring that the audience cannot easily change its known character) made its reappearance whenever there were repertoire seasons. Audiences were secure and exploitable. The enlarged West End, added to the new ring of suburban theatres, meant that the total of major London theatres, 56, is larger than at any other time in our period. The total number of seats available in London each night to see programmes of more or less straight drama, 84,034, meant that roughly 10% of London's 6,528,454 population could have gone to some form of theatre in London every week. Admittedly in the case of the suburban theatres it would have been somewhat dubious fare, as the staple diet of melo-drama and farce had neither the technical values of the West End nor the rough excitement of the early Victorian popular theatres; the stalls did not dress up, but did not 'join in' the entertainment either.

The West End catered of course for a part of this audience, and as an absolute maximum only some 4% of London's population could have gone to the West End theatres weekly. And in every sense West End theatre-going was different from suburban theatre-going. It cost more— a stall seat in the leading suburban theatres was 5s. but more than twice that sum in the West End. In the suburbs tickets were more usually bought at the theatre, and a considerable part of the house

Figure 5

London Theatres 1900

(The following were the major theatres running a substantial programme of straight drama in 1900.)

West End	**Major Suburban (and other) London Theatres**
Adephi	Alexandra, Stoke Newington
Avenue	Brittania, Hoxton
Comedy	Brixton Theatre
Criterion	Broadway, New Cross
Daly's	Court, Sloane Square
Drury Lane	Coronet, Notting Hill
Duke of York's	Crown, Peckham
Gaiety	Dalston
Garrick	Duchess, Balham
Globe	Elephant and Castle
Haymarket	Fulham Grand
Her Majesty's	Grand, Clapham
Imperial	Lyric, Hammersmith
Lyceum	New, Ealing
Lyric	Novelty, Holborn
Olympic	Morton, Greenwich
Prince of Wales's	Old Vic
Princess's	Pavilion, Stepney
Savoy	Princess of Wales, Kennington
Shaftsbury	Richmond New Royal
St. James's	Royal Artillery, Woolwich
Terry's	Royal County, Kingston
Vaudeville	Royalty, Soho
Wyndham's	Sadler's Wells
	Shakespeare, Battersea
Total seats 32,215 approx.	Standard, Shoreditch
	Stratford, Royal
Average Capacity 1,288	Surrey Theatre, Lambeth
	Terriss, Rotherhithe
	Victoria, Walthamstow
	West London

Total seats 51,819 approx.

Average Capacity 1,672

filled from sales at the door; in the West End the rituals of booking one's seat at the elegant 'libraries' were an important part of the experience. In the West End the audiences dressed up—the stalls almost invariably formally dressed as for dinner—and in the suburbs ordinary dress was the rule. Above all there was about the newly self-confident West End a sense of occasion; managers, actors and celebrities in the audience were all national, not local figures, and their activities were respectfully reported as being of general significance.

The managers were now in a highly-ranked and esteemed profession. Managements were long and comfortable—and a manager tended to settle in to a theatre for such a time that his name became associated with it (whether he were an actor or not). Among such long stays are those of George Alexander at the St. James's theatre from 1891-1899, Beerbohm Tree's periods first at the Haymarket (1888-1896) and then at His Majesty's (1897-1917), Augustus Harris at Drury Lane from 1879 to 1897, and Covent Garden from 1888-1896, Charles Hawtrey's seven years at the Comedy (1888-1893, then 1896-1898) and Charles Wyndham's total of twenty four years, first at the Criterion (1879-1889) and then at Wyndham's (1889-1903). Essentially the West End existed as a form of social contract between an elite of some twenty to thirty West End managers and an affluent, influential audience who either naturally enjoyed, or taught themselves to enjoy, the new refinement of theatre-going. Its essence was that the fare on stage was predictable and unsurprising. The same players—Tree, Hicks, Wyndham, Hawtrey, Irene Vanbrugh—played familiar kinds of roles for familiar managers in familiar pieces. The West End playwright could then (as now) sometimes succeed in filling several theatres with his (very recognisable) work, once that style had been accepted. Thus Somerset Maugham anticipated the later success of Noel Coward in having, by 1908, four plays running simultaneously in the West End—*Lady Frederick, Jack Straw, Mrs Dot* and *The Explorer* which together could draw a maximum of 35,000 people a week. In this period too we first see the phenomenon of the 'annual revival', in which a tried and tested piece is regularly re-staged each year for its own established audience. *The Scarlet Pimpernel* was an early example. In 1905 it achieved a run of 123 performances at the New theatre. At the same venue it played 120 performances 12 months later, 224 performances in 1907, 112 in 1908, 154 in 1910, and five years later still ran for 127 performances when it was given a wartime revival, at the Strand.

Figure 6

Attendances at Long-Running Productions 1890s

Show	Theatre	Capacity	No. of Perfs	Total attendance assuming 75%
An Artist's Model	Daly's	994	392	292,236
Charley's Aunt	Royalty	657	1,466	722,371
La Cigale	Lyric	1306	423	414,328
Circus Girl	Gaiety	1126	497	419,716
The Dancing Girl	Haymarket	1159	310	269,467
Dream Faces	Garrick	773	335	194,216
Floradora	Lyric	1306	455	445,672
A Gaiety Girl	Prince of Wales's	960	413	297,360
The Gay Lord Quex	Garrick	773	300	173,925
The Gay Parisienne	Duke of York's	950	369	262,912
The Geisha	Daly's	994	760	566,580
Gentleman Joe	Prince of Wales's	960	392	282,240
Greek Slave	Daly's	994	349	260,179
Little Christopher Columbus	Lyric	1306	361	353,599
The Little Minister	Haymarket	1159	320	278,160
Lord and Lady Algy	Comedy	1055	306	242,122
A Message From Mars	Avenue	1500	544	612,000
The New Boy	Terry's	888	437	291,042
A Night Out	Vaudeville	740	531	294,705
A Pantomime Rehearsal	Terry's	888	439	292,374
La Poupie	Prince of Wales's	960	576	414,720
A Runaway Girl	Gaiety	1126	593	500,788
The Sign of the Cross	Lyric	1306	435	426,082
Walker's London	Toole's	600	511	229,950
What Happened to Jones?	Strand	1250	383	359,062

We cannot of course with any certainty calculate the precise size of the core West End audience because we do not know, first, how many transients visited the London theatre in the 1890s and who, as overseas or provincial visitors, distort the apparent audience figures. Second, we do not know with what *frequency* people went to the theatre. Such descriptions that we have only suggest that the West End audience was mature, and contained a high proportion of women in the more expensive seats. In the stalls, said Henry James, 'the number of old ladies one has to squeeze past is very striking' [7] — to be expected, perhaps, when more than forty per cent of women over 21 were single, and the theatre was one of the few places to which they could go. Descriptions do not however say how many 'regulars' there were.

Yet a very broad indication may be given by the information available. If we assume, for example, that there existed some kind of 'core' audience of West End theatre-goers who would normally visit a smash hit at least once, then the total attendances at the longest running shows gives us a rough upper limit for the audience. In figure 6 are listed all the shows which in the 1890s ran for more than 300 performances, and, assuming their attendances averaged 75% of capacity during the run, a calculation is made in each case of the 'total attendance'. These figures show a wide variation, from 173,925 to 722,371, and the average is 355,832. Such a figure is, obviously, highly notional but it is of credible size for a regular 'core' West End audience—an audience that went to most successes, and whose numbers were swelled, in the case of a cult success such as *Charley's Aunt*, by occasional visitors, transients and by folk visiting the show twice. It would also seem at all events feasible when we consider it in terms of the known total capacity of West End theatres. Again assuming an average 75% of capacity, there were 193,290 seats filled each week in the 1890s, which suggests, not unreasonably, that each member of our supposed 'core' audience went to the theatre, on average, once a fortnight.

It is easier to be certain about the size of the manager's side of the equation. In 1894 a new Theatrical Managers' Association was formed, [8] in which 129 theatres throughout the country were represented, but one in which West End managers were in the minority. These were the only London managers in the association:

West End

Queens	Sir Arthur Butt

Drury Lane	Sir Arthur Butt and Arthur Collins
Garrick	Andre Charlot
Gaiety	Robert Evett
Apollo	E. Laurillard
Winter Garden ⎫	
His Majesty's ⎬	Grossmith and Malone
Shaftesbury ⎭	
Lyceum ⎫	
Princes ⎭	Walter and Frederick Melville
Court	George Dance
Comedy	J. E. Vedrenne

Suburban

Grand, Croydon	B. Blaiberg
Borough, Stratford ⎫	
Theatre Royal, Stratford ⎭	Fred Fredericks
Brixton Theatre	Frederick Melville
Royal Artillery, Woolwich	F. R. Littler

Fewer than a quarter of London's management were represented, but among West End managers in particular the association did not, at the turn of the century, inspire much enthusiasm.

However, on the 20th February, 1908, an organisation was created which is of much greater interest to students of London theatre than the TMA. It was at a private luncheon, held at the Hyde Park Hotel, and to which only a small and select coterie had been invited, that Sir Charles Wyndham created the Association of West End London Managers—a title subsequently shortened to the Society of West End Theatres, or SWET. This body had 22 members, including Sir Charles himself, voted the first President and two honorary members, John Hare and Sir Squire Bancroft. Their names are given in Appendix II.

The new organisation existed to safeguard the interests and the supremacy of the West End theatre. Its new members all resigned from the TMA, and paid an 'entrance fee' of 20 guineas per member. They did not, from the first, admit of any general right to membership from other London managers but kept to themselves the right to add to their numbers only when they chose to do so. On 29th March of that year they became a private Limited Liability Company. However, in order that they could all share the profits from joint advertising, they also created a Joint Stock Company, and the two organisations ran in tandem.

Their early activities with regard to the newspaper advertisements for West End theatre show quite clearly the new Association's use of its own power. They acted first to create an advertising closed shop, insisting that all members must advertise in the same manner, by being listed

106

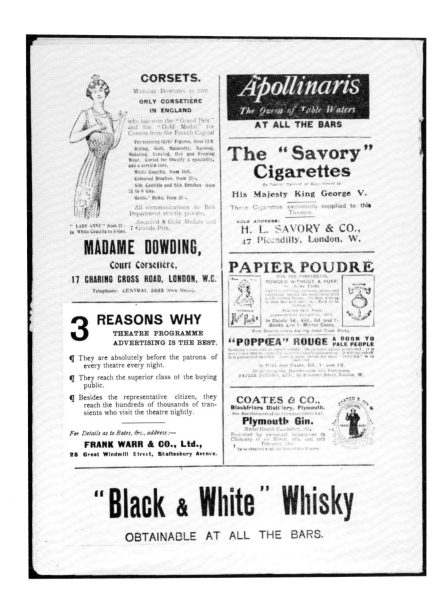
The fashionable Wyndham's Theatre made no bones about its
audience - the 'superior class of the buying public'.

each day in the newspapers with (usually) a four-line entry. Second, they acted to emphasise the exclusivity of the West End and, with their new collective power, were able to insist that in newspapers such as the *Westminster Gazette* and the *Pall Mall Gazette*, where theatre advertising had been scattered through the paper, West End advertising must in future be gathered together and displayed in dignified fashion, well away from that of other theatres. The Association was prepared to use its power on other newspapers too. When the *Evening News* failed to offer a proper discount for their regular patronage, members united to withdraw their advertising and, quite soon, forced the Editor to climb down and offer the same kind of terms as the other publications, 3s. per two-line insert, which they accepted. And when, during that first summer, the manager of the Queen's Theatre, Courtnedge, rashly placed an advertisement in the *Daily Mail* without consulting his colleagues, the minutes carry the somewhat threatening message that one of their number 'was requested to call on Mr. Courtnedge . . .'

Thus, through the turn of the century and into the Edwardian Era the West End theatre was firmly established in its location, its practices and its status. It generated and lived out its own myths, standing invariably for the 'best theatre' for the best people. It was prosperous—although its prices were higher, relative to a common working class wage, than ever before or since (see Appendix III). But it was scarcely *popular*. Its audiences were loyal and well-to-do, but even at its zenith the fashionable West End was not as popular in the numerical sense as were the music halls. It was involved in a muted, somewhat righteous way by its well-mannered clientele, but did not generate the easy and unaffected popularity for its stars that was given to sporting heroes. It was the kind of experience suggested by many of the prints of Edwardian actors and Edwardian theatre audiences—a slightly formal, ritualised occasion—more than a dash of boredom spent in company which, if it were not distinguished, at least dressed in a manner that suggested it might be.

Both sides of the footlights were, one might say, conscious of being professional—both in the sense that they were above ordinary trade, and in the sense of carrying responsibilities. The solemn rituals of snobbery, which Thackeray had taken pains to describe, [9] extended far beyond the reaction to the play and involved the dressing-up, the gathering together of the theatre party, the dining out, the foyer conversation, and the care in saying the 'correct' thing afterwards. It was indeed the period when West End theatre, in all senses, fully professionalised itself. By a reflex action, the amateur movement also organised itself more thoroughly. A number of major amateur dramatic societies were formally constituted at this time—C. B. Purdom began Letchworth Dramatic Society in 1906, Edwin T. Hays began Stockport Garrick Society in 1905, and in 1911 the People's Theatre, Newcastle-upon-Tyne was formed. Even earlier, in 1899 the National Operatic and Dramatic Association had been formed to bring the growing number of amateur societies into formal federation. With a very few exceptions however, amateur societies made no attempt to revive earlier and simpler theatrical styles, but became decorous imitators of West End practices. They bought from Lacy's and, after 1881, they bought from Samuel French, 'acting editions' which enabled them to copy slavishly not merely the script of a West End success, but its properties, its setting and furniture, its 'moves' and even some of the gestures and inflections of the West End actors.

Thus the West End settled into its comfortable professionalism, its acting style perpetuated, after its foundation in 1904, by the Royal Academy of Dramatic Art, and its managerial practices perpetuated by families and by well-to-do London club members who were of that exclusive theatrical fraternity. And in the provinces, the touring theatres played an endless succession of 'West End successes', while the amateur societies acted out, in a sad parody of smartness, the brittle epigrams of Mayfair on the stages of a thousand village halls.

Theatrical inbreeding. Armistice Night, a scene in Noel Coward's West End success 'Cavalcade'. The celebrations are set in the West End, with a bus advertising the West End's biggest First World War success.

9
In Defence of
Good Breeding
1918-1939

'Let's drink to the spirit of gallantry and courage that made a strange Heaven out of unbelievable Hell, and let's drink to the hope that one day this country of ours, which we love so much, will find dignity and greatness and peace again.'

Noel Coward, Cavalcade 1931

When the West End theatres reopened, a few weeks after the outbreak of the First World War, there was a feeling of mild indignation in the writings of the London establishment, as if above all else the war were to be deplored because it brought so many signs of ill-breeding. As G. B. Hibbert said:

'A curious difference became apparent in the personnel of the audiences. The regular, known, patron of the theatres seemed to disappear. In his place came strangers, constant in mutation— cosmopolitan visitors to town, soldiers home on leave, mainly anxious, it seemed, to kill time under any cover and, if they paid any attention to the performance, caring most for inane, vulgar and often indecent revue, or crude and unlifelike studies of warfare.' [1]

Hibbert's bemused wonderment at the 'curious' difference a world war makes to the fashionable theatre, and his bewilderment that some of the regular, *known* patrons had other things to do than take their accustomed seats in the stalls, pales into insignificance beside his accusation that soldiers on leave had the wretched taste to prefer *unlifelike* studies of war—in the midst of the carnage of the trenches, the final and authoritative view of what was lifelike thus came from a deep armchair somewhere in London's clubland.

There is however no doubt that the effect of the war years was to bring back at least temporarily some of the raw edge of entertainment to the mannered theatres. Song and dance tended to replace the epigram on London's stages and, for obvious reasons, the male dominance of the cast lists was reversed: musicals and revues gained a strong new hold on the West End. Some were immediately profitable. The first revue, *Odds and Ends*, which opened at the Ambassadors theatre in 1914, cost £200 to stage, and made a profit of £30,000 on its 376 performances. More profitable still was *Chu Chin Chow*, a musical which was originally conceived as a Christmas entertainment, which cost £5,300 to stage at His Majesty's theatre in 1916, including £1,439 on wages and materials for the scenery, £1,858 on costumes and £335 on properties, and, with running costs averaging throughout its run some £200, had by the end of its 2,238 performances made its presenter Oscar Asche a profit of £100,000. Once a show established itself in wartime London, the high mutation of cosmopolitan visitors anxious 'to kill time under any cover' frequently ensured a long run. *Romance*, which opened at the Duke of York's in 1915, ran for 1,045 performances (although a revival in 1926, when things were more settled, at the Playhouse, ran for only 131) and *Maid of the Mountains*, which opened at Daly's in 1917, ran for 1,352.

At the end of the war there was a considerable change in the managerial structure of the West End. By 1918 the actor managers who had formerly dominated the establishment theatre, Irving, Tree, Alexander and Wyndham, were all dead. In Philip Godfrey's words:

'The end of the war, with its economic uncertainties, completed the shuffling of the pack, and left the company promoter on top. Theatrical syndicates had been formed to buy up every theatre as it came on the market, and as a monopoly in theatres approached rents began to soar to scandalous heights. Theatres which had been let at £50 a week when they were sold, now cost ten times that price, and many actor-managers who had left the theatre temporarily during the war were thus prevented from coming back into business, or, with such a financial handicap, could only do so disastrously.' [2]

There was nothing new about syndicates either owning theatres or running production companies, but what was new was the fact that many new businessmen of uncertain theatrical pedigree entered management, at a time of inflationary rents, and this added to the belief

His Majesty's Theatre

Licensee   J. D. LANGTON

OSCAR ASCHE AND LILY BRAYTON
SEASON

NEW SONGS   NEW DANCES

NEW SCENES   NEW COSTUMES

and

NEW CHARACTERS

CHU CHIN CHOW

A MUSICAL TALE OF THE EAST

Told by OSCAR ASCHE

and

Set to Music by FREDERIC NORTON

The long-running Chu Chin Chow was regularly revamped for its audiences - including the addition of new dialogue, new situations and new characters.

Figure 7

Rateable Value of London's Theatres 1911-1921

	1911 £	1921 £
Adelphi	4,875	5,000
Aldwych	3,750	3,750
Apollo	4,584	4,584
Ambassadors	—	1,667
Comedy	3,700	3,750
Criterion	2,917	3,334
Court	1,167	1,000
Covent Garden	4,959	5,625
Daly's	5,125	5,417
Drury Lane	5,834	6,215
Duke of York's	3,750	3,750
Gaiety	5,834	5,834
Globe	4,792	4,792
Garrick	4,167	4,167
Haymarket	4,500	4,584
His Majesty's	5,813	5,834
Kingsway	834	1,250
Little	1,200	1,334
Lyric	4,584	4,584
London Opera House	7,000	7,500
Lyceum	4,584	5,000
New	3,750	3,750
Playhouse	3,395	3,334
Prince of Wales's	4,584	4,584
Prince's	1,615	2,084
Queen's	4,792	4,792
Royalty	1,500	1,500
St. James's	3,750	4,167
Savoy	2,500	2,500
Scala	—	774
Shaftsbury	4,167	4,584
Strand	3,809	4,167
Vaudeville	2,500	2,751
Wyndham's	3,500	3,750
St. Martin's	—	2,292

that some of the personalised contact between the managers and their known audience was lost. There was a sense that the West End was in danger of once more reverting to *trade*. This was heightened by the fact that some purchasers had international interests; for example Metro Goldwyn bought the old Empire theatre in Leicester Square in 1921, and opened it in 1928 as the Empire, Leicester Square, Cinema, and in 1923 opened a cinema in the Strand which was constructed on the site of the Tivoli, which they had bought in 1919.

It has also to be said that many of the former theatre owners, who had built in the boom years around the turn of the century, were very ready to sell. Beerbohm Tree had, for example, made several attempts to sell His Majesty's Theatre. When it was sold, after his death, to Grossmith and Laurillard, it made £110,000, a good profit on the £70,000 Tree had spent on its purchase and redevelopment in 1897. The purchasers did not however either represent any sinister new foreign intruder, nor any coarse new commercial syndicate, but merely represented a north countryman with an interest in theatre. Although some people no doubt bought theatres for base commercial reasons, the ownership of a theatre building was not a guarantee of wealth[3]. According to Hibbert, it actually cost £7,000 a year, for instance, to run His Majesty's Theatre—in ground rent, insurance, building costs and rates. And rates had indeed risen during the war, although, as Figure 7 shows, not by the huge percentages of later years.

It was in the years following the first World War that the 'split'—the agreement to divide the box-office receipts between the management owning the theatre and the management producing the play—became a matter of contention. If theatre owners found the post-war costs of maintaining and lighting a building high—Charles Wyndham's widow, Mary Moore, who succeeded him in management, had to economise on costs when she housed Noel Coward's first London play, and removed half the lighting during its faltering five week run—then the producing managements in their turn protested that their costs had risen just as much and they were now being asked to agree to impossible 'splits', which either gave owners a high guaranteed rental, or too high a proportion of the receipts.

Production costs certainly did rise. It was not uncommon for a musical now to cost over £10,000 to stage, and a straight play might easily cost £3,000. The West End star could soon expect to be earning a weekly three figure salary. In his 1980 autobiography *Up In The Clouds*

Gentlemen Please, John Mills recounts how his salary as an 'unknown', £15 a week, rose rapidly when he became a star, until in 1934 he was earning £150 a week. To meet such escalating costs backers or 'angels' had to be found in greater numbers.

The backer was not a new phenomenon; in 1872 the luckless Lord Londesborough had lost nearly £100,000 in backing Dion Boucicault's *Babel and Bijou* at Covent Garden. There were however new characteristics of backing productions. First, you did so more usually now as a part of a group or syndicate, who would expect not only to agree to a 'second call' on their funds if mounting the production proved more expensive than at first expected, but who would also expect to be given a voice in shaping the production at its 'try out' stage. There was considerable unease over the new syndicates of backers, and over the influence of 'angels' as a class, as Philip Godfrey makes clear:

> 'Anyone who had studied the problems of providing the financial backing for a play knows that backers fall into three classes. First there is a small class of wealthy people who have a genuine interest in the theatre and who are prepared to put up the expenses if they feel the play is worth it. This rare type of backer is not primarily interested in profits, and is even ready to lose money to sponsor good dramatic art. The ordinary company promoter cannot reach this class, as he does not understand its ideas nor speak its culture idiom.
>
> 'The second, and principal source of supply comes from a class of wealthy business-men who like a 'long shot' in speculation, and are prepared to risk a few thousands in the hopes of finding a winner which may return their money a hundredfold. Their interest is confined to the box-office, and their participation in theatre matters mostly results in a series of costly failures.
>
> 'The third class of backers is those who (to quote the professional term) take a bedroom interest in the theatre. Wealthy men who are interested in actresses, apart from their acting, or rich women who take a similar interest in actors, will sponsor plays provided only that there is a leading part for the women of their fancy.' [4]

Writing in 1933, and looking back over the years since the war, Godfrey paints a picture of post-war uncertainty; once the bond between the middle class audience and the revitalised pre-war West End theatre had been weakened, there was a loss of confidence by the managers in their own taste, and a good many 'intrusive personal elements'. In addition to the backers with a bedroom interest, he cites managers with mistresses or second wives who act, 'One doting manager, who does not act, has lost £70,000 during the last five years in trying out plays with suitable leading parts for his (second) wife', and the dangers from the actor friends of backers who 'make it a condition that in exchange for their money they shall receive a part to play [5]. He is particularly scornful of the new manager's blind belief in 'American methods' of publicity, which have convinced him that 'if only his advertising is sensational enough he will be sure to recoup his expenditure and clear a profit. Consequently he will set aside large sums for publicity which he would never dream of spending to make his production better, his auditorium more comfortable, or in searching for new creative intelligence'. [6]

Such strictures do not apply to all West End management, because it lost some of its former homogeniety after 1914. There *were* backers of disinterested generosity like Barry Jackson, whose willingness to finance personally the expensive five parts of *Back to Methuselah* caused Shaw anxiously to enquire, 'Jackson, are you certain your wife and children are insured?' There were financial successes for the small-scale and homely, like *Journey's End*, which made its author R. C. Sherrif an immediate £20,000 when it was produced in 1929. There were some innovative departures, ranging from such extraordinary C. B. Cochran shows as *The League of Notions* at the Oxford in 1921, which cost £30,000 to stage and resembled the early Victorian spectaculars, to small-scale pieces of social realism, such as the D. H. Lawrence play *The Widowing of Mrs Holroyd* produced in 1926, which may be said to antedate the social realism of the 1960s. But there remained some general characteristics still in presentation. Most of the social rituals associated with West End theatre-going remained, albeit in modified form. The stalls dressed formally for the West End theatre and for the opera, and both were after-dinner diversions for the regulars. Plays now began later, often at eight-thirty, so that Londoners who had formerly been prevented from attending because they worked too late were now sometimes prevented from attending because they had no private transport available to take them home after the show. Division of classes within the theatre was still marked.

On stage, the new vulgarity combined with the old refinement to produce a characteristic kind of between-the-wars drama. Shows had a brittle new sophistication, which was inward-looking, and which fed upon its own personalities and its own West End theatrical lore. Productions were no longer constrained by the manners and values of an identifiable London middle class, but created instead a new hybrid of innocence and world-weariness, which reached its zenith with the work of Ivor Novello. Novello, whose West End appearances ranged from straight dramas such as *The Rat* to the vast Drury Lane musicals such as *Glamorous Night* and *Careless Rapture*, made £178,000 (before tax) from his work between 1928 and 1939, and also made, as the ubiquitous Macqueen-Pope wrote, 'an approach of his own, an epoch of truly British shows when they were most needed'. [7]

Off-stage, it was an epoch in which the West End managements were threatened by competition, and Novello's high profits were exceptional. It is the way in which the managers, old and new, rallied to meet that competition which ensured that the West End would remain, for all its uncertainties and ostensible changes in style, essentially an insular and secretive oligarchy. Threatened by an upsurge of provincial theatre, by the cinema, the radio, and by a significant new 'art' theatre movement in London, those figures that met at the Garrick, or the Green Room, or at 52 Shaftsbury Avenue, invariably decided at each stage to take refuge in the social status that had been won for them at the end of the nineteenth century, and reacted to each commercial threat with a strangely Victorian *hauteur* which implied that they were still above *trade*, and that thoughts of co-operating with other commercial interests or sharing new markets with different kinds of competitor were equally repugnant to men of their rank.

Although the 130 established provincial theatres on the regular circuits continued to present try-outs 'prior to London', or plays 'following the successful West End run' with, allegedly 'established London favourites' in them, there were signs of a falling away of business, particularly in the Number 2 venues. There was in the thirties a new emphasis in provincial theatre advertising which, controlled from London, attempted to shore up London's pre-eminence. In particular following the 1932 slump, touring plays were advertised as being '*Immediately* prior to West End production', '*Direct* from the West End', with 'the *Full* London Company'.

Most markedly, the established touring theatres suffered from the competition of the growing band of provincial repertory companies. In the early thirties there were companies officially affiliated to the repertory movement in Birmingham, Bristol, Hull, Liverpool, Manchester, Northampton, Plymouth, Rochester, Southend and Sheffield; by 1939 the number had grown to forty. Their significance was not just in their location, but in the notions of service which informed their management. The repertory system meant that they were not seeking to present long runs, but a regularly varied programme. Their position in provincial centres meant that there was a good deal more involvement by local people in their work—through playgoers' societies, discussion groups, work with local schools and colleges, theatre club meetings and the like—which prevented them from simply aping the West End theatre. There was a considerable amateur involvement in their work, which meant that although the actors would usually come from elsewhere, the theatre board, the manager, many of the stage crew and the box-office and house staff were likely to be local people with strong local interests at heart.

A year's programme at any of the major provincial repertory companies was impressively different from the kind of programme that would be housed in the touring theatre with whom they were in competition; it was markedly more international, more literary and more innovative. William Armstrong, who had been director of Liverpool Rep. since 1923 and whose policy had included the performance in each season of at least 12 new one-act plays by untried dramatists, said at the outbreak of the Second World War:

> 'For years we were financially successful, and in spite of weekly expenses of £500, made a regular profit. But this miracle was not achieved by deserting rep. and exploiting London successes. Some of our biggest financial successes were plays like Sherwood's *The Road to Rome*, Sierra's *The Kingdom of God*, Schauffler's *Parnell*, Priestley's *Time and the Conways* and Huxley's *The World of Light*. We made money on all our Shakespearian productions.' [8]

There were similar successes for ventures as different as Terence Gray's Festival theatre in Cambridge and John Moore's Bridie productions at Tewkesbury. Some companies, like Sheffield, played complete seasons of new foreign drama. Others, like Birmingham, became associated in particular with one dramatist. Cedric Hardwicke describes his interview with Barry Jackson who, as heir to the Maypole Dairies, was able to spend some £200,000 in promoting his Birmingham Repertory Company, and the major house dramatist, G. B. Shaw:

'Barry Jackson's opening words to me at our original meeting prompted me to lie. 'Are you interested in George Bernard Shaw? You won't like it here if you aren't.'

'It has been impressed upon me by older heads than mine that you must never disappoint a manager. I should have confessed unblushingly, had I been asked, that I could sing, dance, train lions, or walk a tight-rope. 'Rath-*er!*' I replied to Mr Jackson, but my lie brought me no immediate results.

'Let me think about it and let you know,' he said, after a brief and vague interview. I recalled enough of the old days to recognise this as a polite farewell.' [9]

Hardwicke's subsequent career—he was, a month later, taken into the company, and became a favoured actor in G. B. Shaw's plays—illustrates one important aspect of the way the repertory companies came to fit into the career structure of actors. As payment in the reps was less than that in London, as the reps rarely received the kind of press coverage which furthers an actor's career, and as provincial work rarely allowed actors the opportunity of working in films, radio and—later—television in ways that would enhance their prospects, it was quickly accepted that the reps were not centres of excellence in their own right, but *training centres* for, ultimately, London work. The West End establishment accepted such a view readily; more sadly, the reps did too, and were wont to boast more of the eminent actors who had got their 'start' with them, rather than those excellent players who stayed, and who did not acquire London reputations.

The new reps, and new uncommercial touring groups such as the Arts League of Service, meant that provincials saw more classic work than London, where, with the exception of the productions at the Old Vic, even Shakespeare was rarely seen. There was too a massive resurgence of amateur drama. A publisher, Geoffrey Whitworth, was instrumental in calling the first national conference of the British Drama League in 1919. By 1923 some 300 amateur societies were affiliated to it, by 1930 there were 1,600, and by the late thirties the number had grown to 3,000. By that time it was a reasonable estimate that there were a quarter of a million amateur actors and actresses in Britain, although few groups were innovative.

The threat to the West End's dominance of British drama loomed larger on two other fronts—the growth of the cinema, and the emergence of broadcasting. The reaction of the West End managers in each case was one of affronted anger, compounded equally of suspicions that both their position as arbiters of sophisticated drama, and their financial monopoly, were at risk.

The Society of West End Managers had as early as 1911 recorded their fears that the burgeoning film industry was a threat to their business, and on July 5th had passed a resolution which said:

a) That in the opinion of this Society the giving of facilities to the Managers of Picture Palace Theatres enabling them to take cinematograph records, or films, and so to reproduce theatrical performances, is very prejudicial to the general interests of the theatrical profession and is accordingly greatly to be deprecated.

b) this society trusts that members will accordingly refrain from giving any such facilities.

The threat however was not to be contained by simply refusing film producers access to the theatres. Original scripts were filmed in the industry's own studios, and the growing industry was able to attract West End stars to appear for high salaries; Tree, who was persuaded to appear with his company in an early Ealing film of *Henry VIII*, was paid £1,000 for his services. The growth of the exhibiting companies throughout Britain was equally rapid. In 1908 there were three companies with £110,000 capital, and by 1911, when S.W.E.T.M. solemnly announced the exclusion of the managers of picture palaces from their precincts, there were more than 300, with nearly £3,500,000 capital.

The growth of both studios and cinemas in London was particularly rapid. The first house to present an exclusive film programme in London was the Balham Empire in 1907. Five years later the *London Evening News* commented with some awe that there were now some 500 cinemas in London, each employing, on average, a staff of eight. The 50 or so purpose-built cinemas in central London fed off the glamour and excitement which the theatre managers had sought to give the area. They were built with interiors remarkably like the fashionable West End theatres—sometimes designed by men who, like Frank Matcham, had made early reputations as theatre architects—with one important difference. In the new cinemas all seating was good and comfortable, and even in those cinemas in which there was differential pricing, the cheaper seats were a great deal more comfortable than their (slightly more expensive) equivalents in the theatres. Significantly, when there was differential pricing, the cheaper cinema seats were those *nearest* to the action, as had been the case in the popular theatre of the 1840s and 1850s.

In general, the cinema was much cheaper than the theatre, for the cinema manager had lower costs. His capital costs were in any case lower, for the building of a cinema was less expensive than the more ornate building that was now necessary for a theatre, with its small, separated areas for the different segments of the audience; no cinema, for example, in central London cost as much to build as the Fortune, which opened in 1924, and cost three times its estimated cost to build. The cinema manager had, in addition, far lower hiring costs for films than the costs of staging a live show, and had lower staff costs, as the less complicated cinema auditoriums cost much less to run. Prices of admission were in general therefore very low. 'Bottom' prices of 3d., 4d. and 6d. were fairly common in all but the central London cinemas.

In central London the newly built cinemas engaged in a curious competition with the West End theatre. Not only did they copy their 'artistic' format, with carpeted lounges and foyers, uniformed flunkeys, and select refreshment areas, but they emphasised their status by charging high prices for their film premieres, and for the showing of 'first run' films. Thus the Regent Street Poly charged 10s. 6d. top price, and the Marble Arch Pavilion 11s. 6d. Most interestingly, one cinema, known at the time of writing as the Rialto, Coventry Street, which simply called itself the 'West End Theatre', even charged a 'top' price of 21s., more than virtually any theatre price in London.

As the competition from the growing cinema industry intensified, the TMA joined SWET in uneasy partnership in expressing alarm. In 1923 Sydney Cooper insisted to his fellow members that any filmed version of a play would inevitably have a disastrous effect upon member's theatres. In their various interviews and public expostulations the theatre managers fell back upon the insistence that they were 'art', that they knew all about acting, and that the cinemas represented some new, vulgar and bogus commodity. The actor Fred Kerr announced for example that he could not for the life of him share the enthusiasm of the public for well-known film stars, and moreover added, 'I intensely resent their being invariably alluded to as actors and actresses'. In contrast to the higher theatrical art of the West End, the cinema was base commercialism. It had a certain entertainment value of course, 'if only we could be spared the ravings of the press about its artistry'.

It was however the popular variety theatres, the remaining suburban

Figure 8

British Theatre Attendance 1918-24

	Admissions	Tax Yield	Percentage Increase/Decrease
1918/19	592,016,720	£7,400,009	-
1919/20	813,652,960	£10,170,662	37.4 +
1920/21	938,867,200	£11,735,840	15.4 +
1921/22	822,363,440	£10,279,543	12.4 −
1922/23	768,243,760	£9,603,047	6.6 −
1923/24	724,586,640	£9,057,333	5.7 −

theatres, and the cheaper parts of the West End theatre which suffered most from the competition. As Kerr points out:

'There can be little doubt that the cheaper parts of the theatre have suffered considerably from the popularity of the cinema; it is regrettable, though unavoidable. But theatres would make a better fight for themselves if they were half as comfortable as most picture-houses are.' [10]

Regrettably however there is little evidence that the theatre managers wished to compete with the cinema for the popular audience, and no evidence that they decided to make the cheaper part of a theatre more welcoming or more comfortable. The impact of the cinema upon their attendances (before 1924, when the radio began transmitting drama and thus brought a new element into the competition) is shown in Figure 8; unfortunately the decline in attendances was not sufficient to force theatre managers to re-examine policy, and to return to a less elitist practice.

The theatre's disadvantage was in the event compounded by the Entertainments Tax, which was levied upon all places of entertainment in 1916 and which was supposedly a temporary measure, although in fact it remained in being for half a century. There was combined opposition to it after the war from both theatre and cinema managers. Unfortunately, when relief did come, in 1924, it was in the form of an abolition of tax on all seats up to 6d. in price, and a lessening of the tax on all seats up to 1s. 3d. Such a change plainly was to the cinemas' advantage, for they still had many seats priced below 6d. and an even larger number priced at less than 1s. 3d. The majority of theatre tickets cost much more than that, and therefore the theatres gained no relief, and the cinema managers a considerable boost.

A further, minor, advantage which the new cinemas enjoyed was simply that they did not adhere to the Edwardian notion of opening only in the evening and for occasional matinees. They were almost always open from noon, and many London ones opened in mid-morning. They were therefore places in which the leisured, the shift-worker and the growing army of unemployed could sit in comfort during the day, without dressing up, and without the social complexity of booking in advance at fashionable 'libraries'.

Not surprisingly, a number of the larger suburban theatres soon followed the path of the Kilburn Empire. Built as a 2,000 seater venue in 1899 for the staging of circus and music hall, it was by the early twenties regularly interleaving its live presentations with films, and by 1928 had been converted to a full-time cinema.

When in 1928 the 'talkies' arrived in London, and there was a further growth in cinema attendances—there were some 4,000 cinemas by 1930—the attitudes of the theatre managers were fixed. They continued to emphasise that their art had a distinctive social cachet which raised it far above the commonplace popularity of the cinema industry, and they related their traditional audience that responded to a culture that seemed at once to be glamorous and to elevate them as participants in a 'live' art. To see Ivor Novello on stage was socially superior to seeing Ivor Novello on film. The venerated surroundings, and the implied link with London society that attendance at a fashionable theatre gave, meant that the experience was socially uplifting even if one were uncomfortable and could neither hear nor see the actors very well. Through the twenties the cinema industry had tried to ensnare some of this fashionable air—Sir Oswald Stoll even chose to premiere his film version of *The Prodigal Son* in 1923 in the Royal Opera House, in the vain hope that the hallowed walls of one of the patent houses would lend his work the aura of high art—but their attempts were doomed. The most elevated personages in London society continued to lend their presences to the theatre. George V visited the London theatre officially 170 times between 1918 and his death in 1935. By contrast the first official Royal Film Performance did not take place until 1948.

If the cinema posed a threat to the theatre establishment however, then the radio offered an all-out assault. The Marconi Company began broadcasting from Chelmsford in 1920; in 1922, in London, the British

124

Broadcasting Company was created at a meeting attended by more than 200 organisations connected with radio; in 1923, under its new General Manager, John Reith, it obtained government license and became in effect the national broadcasting company, although it did not take the form and title of the present British Broadcasting Corporation until 1926. Its growth was even more rapid than that of the cinema. In 1922 Reith had a staff of four and some 26,000 people possessed radio licences. In 1926 the staff had grown to more than 600 and licence-holders numbered in excess of 2,000,000.

Again, the reaction of the theatre managers was hostile; at the annual general meeting of the T.M.A. in 1923 it was decided that they 'could not give any facilities' to broadcasting, and plainly there was an intention to try to stop drama being broadcast at all. However there was a considerable popular outcry at their stance, and the popular press gave full coverage to the arguments between the managers of the theatres and the new managers of the B.B.Co. There was general approval of the B.B.Co.'s position that there was room for cooperation between them and the theatre managers. The *Sunday Pictorial*, on 29th April 1923, published in detail the B.B.Co.'s arguments:

'The ban which the Theatrical Managers' Association has placed on the broadcasting of plays, music and other entertainments leaves the British Broadcasting Company placid and serene.

'We regret it, but it leaves us unruffled,' said a prominent official yesterday, 'We don't want to fight, but by jingo if we are forced to it we are ready. We are willing to co-operate and work with any existing interests, but if they are averse, then we shall be prepared to discharge our obligations to the public and put on a first-class programme.'

The 'official' spokesman went on to point out, albeit rather clumsily, the glaring weakness of the managers' position:

'I consider there is room for both of us, and we have definite proof that the broadcasting of excerpts from plays, operas and entertainments has resulted in 2,000 seats being booked at the theatres by 'listeners-in'.

People won't go to the theatres every night, and they won't stay at home every night. The attitude of the theatrical managers seems to me to be very short-sighted.'

The managers had in fact no proof, nor indeed any kind of evidence,

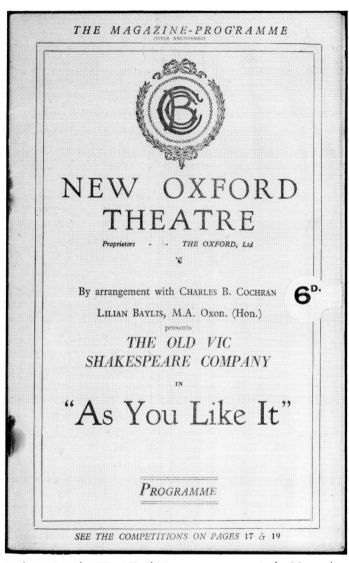

NEW OXFORD
THEATRE

Proprietors - - *THE OXFORD, Ltd*

By arrangement with CHARLES B. COCHRAN

6ᴰ·

LILIAN BAYLIS, M.A. Oxon. (Hon.)

presents

THE OLD VIC
SHAKESPEARE COMPANY

IN

"As You Like It"

PROGRAMME

SEE THE COMPETITIONS ON PAGES 17 & 19

In the 1920s the West End Managers supported a Magazine Programme, which was on sale at 18 West End theatres, having an average sale of 50,000. It contained stage anecdotes, jokes, competitions and some stage biographies.

that broadcasting would affect attendances adversely; it was an instinctive urge to preserve a business and social monopoly, unsupported by research or analysis. As the American actor Edward H. Robins went on to say in the same article:

> 'In America the audience of listeners-in must be ten times as numerous as in this country where, I am told, it totals a million and a half. Yet the idea that broadcasting shows will jeopardise their success has never entered the American managers' heads.'

American theatre management was of course motivated by a straightforward commercial instinct and not, as here, partly by notions of exclusivity and social rank.

In December of the same year the hostility of the managers to the radio reached a new peak. C. B. Cochran (who did not then belong to any managerial association) had made an agreement with the B.B.Co. to broadcast his musical production *Little Nellie Kelly* from the Oxford. Both managerial groups reacted with fury. The T.M.A.'s provincial managers announced that if the broadcast went ahead they would not book its provincial tour because 'its drawing power would be nil', and the S.W.E.T.M. Chairman, Walter Payne, commenced proceedings against the B.B.Co. on behalf of the interests of the West End managers. The result was that the agreement was broken, the broadcast did not take place, and the B.B.Co. actually paid Payne's costs.

However the managers were unable to prevent the B.B.Co. from creating their own drama productions, and in 1924 these began to be presented on a regular basis, a kind of loose quota system being agreed with the theatre managers, supposedly to limit the output. As with the cinema, the radio managers copied aspects of West End presentation, in their case prefacing plays with long overtures, as in the theatre, and of course using West End 'stars'. Between August 1924 and September 1925 149 drama productions were broadcast, and the 'stars' included Lady Forbes Robertson, Lewis Casson, Sybil Thorndike, Mrs Kendall and Lady Tree. And in 1925 the B.B.Co. sealed the fact that radio drama was to be a form separate from traditional theatre by commissioning its first full-length radio play, *The White Chateau* by Reginald Berkeley, which was broadcast on Armistice Day.

Of ultimately greater significance than their initial hostility to cinema and radio drama was the managers' strong, and successful, opposition to the Local Authorities being permitted to levy rates for the purposes of presenting any kind of dramatic entertainment. Until 1925 Local

Authorities had been permitted to raise rate income up to a limit of one penny for entertainment—usually, although not invariably, musical concerts in the parks. Some had exceeded this slightly, amongst them the holiday centres of Bath, Bridlington, Folkestone, Hastings, Lytham St. Annes, Morecambe, Southend-on-Sea, Tunbridge Wells, Filey, the Matlocks, Worthing and Whitby. It was not always easy for Parliament to distinguish expenditure on entertainment in the rates because of the different methods of labelling Local Authority expenditure. By 1925 however some authorities were clearly providing entertainment well above the penny rate. Bath was for example spending an annual £5,898, a rate of 3½d. in the pound, Folkstone was spending £1,400 equivalent to a 1¼d. rate, and Morecombe's expenditure of £2,800 represented an even higher rate of nearly 7d.

A bill was presented to Parliament which sought to give Local Authorities greater freedom in presenting drama, and which at first permitted any Local Authority to spend up to twopence in the pound on entertainments, a figure which could be raised if such action were approved by the Minister of Health. The *1925 Public Health [Amendment] Act* sought in its original form these objectives:

'Any part of the park or ground enclosed under paragraph (b) of Subsection (1) of the principal Section for the purposes of bands of music may be used for any of the purposes of concerts *or other entertainments.*

Any expenditure of the local authority, in the exercise of their powers to provide or contribute to a band under Subsection (1) of the principal Section, and any expenditure of the local authority in the exercise of their powers under Subsection (1) of this Section, shall not, when added together, exceed in any one year an amount equal to that which would be produced by *a rate of twopence in the pound* on the property liable to be assessed for the purpose of the rate out of which the expenses of the park or ground are payable, as assessed for the time being for the purpose of that rate, *or such higher rate in the pound as may be approved by the Minister of Health*, and Subsection (3) of the principal Section shall cease to have effect'. (My italics)

The theatre managers saw at once a serious threat in the somewhat labyrinth proposal. Before the bill was laid before the house backstairs pressure induced the bill's promoters to amend the proposal so that Local Authorities could present dramatic entertainments, if they chose, which cost the equivalent of only a penny rate.

The debate in the House of Commons then centred upon whether the reference to 'other entertainments' should not be replaced by 'band performance'. At their February meeting of that year S.W.E.T.M. had instructed their representative Mr Watney to brief their supporters in the house to support such an amendment, and there was considerable support for the position of the West End managers. Colonel Applin supported the replacement of the phrase 'other entertainments', stressing that 'private enterprise' must be left to run the theatre. Captain Gee put the case even more strongly:

'If we pass this clause the result will be the same as before. People will get something for nothing. Unless you pay for a thing you will not appreciate it, and if people want to go to theatres and music halls they are quite content to save up the money to go.'

This was opposed by Captain Garro-Jones:

'I cannot have any great sympathy for the theatrical or cinema people in this matter. The remedy for them is to reduce their charges, and not to charge 13/6d. for a stall in a West End, and sometimes in an East End, place of amusement.

The net result was that although the bill left the House of Commons with the offending clause intact, it was agreed that an amendment would be moved in its House of Lords reading which would be acceptable to all parties. There was thus a breathing space for the West End managers to apply further pressure to have the clause deleted.

By September Walter Payne was able to report to S.W.E.T.M. that following 'many interviews' with the Minister of Health it had been agreed that the following sentences should be inserted in the bill during its Lords reading:

'Provided that the following restrictions shall have effect with respect to any concert or other entertainment provided by the Local Authority under this section, that is to say—

1 No stage play shall be performed, and
2 The concert or other entertainment shall not include any performance in the nature of a variety entertainment, and
3 No cinematograph film, other than a film illustrative of questions relating to health or disease shall be shown, and
4 No scenery, theatrical costumes or scenic or theatrical accessories shall be used.

Not surprisingly this virtual endorsement of the *status quo* was 'considered extremely satisfactory' by the members, and Payne was 'thanked for his work in the matter'.

There was however one further disturbing trend which was almost as worrying as the success of the repertory movement and the threat by the local authorities to include the drama in their notion of public amenities. This was the growth of the small theatres in London which sought to find special audiences for new forms of theatre. The trend was not of course entirely new—Grein and Archer's Independent theatre had presented 50 productions of high literary quality between 1899 and 1909—but its scale and success both were. The Mercury theatre at Notting Hill, for example, which had been founded by the investment of the £10,000 which Ashley Dukes had made from *The Man with a Load of Mischief*, was able to run T. S. Eliot's *Murder in the Cathedral* for nine months, playing to 20,000 people. Ronald Adam, who started his Embassy, Swiss Cottage, management on a capital of £87, produced a hundred (mostly new) plays there between 1932 and 1936, and there was activity on a similar scale at theatres such as the Arts, the Unity and L. M. Lion's 'Q' theatre at Kew. The financial advantage the small theatres had was that many of their workers were voluntary or part-time helpers, so the bill for all kinds of running costs was much lower than that of the West End theatres. Adam, for instance, says that his total costs, theatre and play, for running a production at the 678-seater Embassy theatre in Swiss Cottage were less than £500 a week. The final advantage for the small theatres was that the West End establishment began to relinquish the word 'art' and replace it with 'glamour'; it was the glamorous theatre, not simply the artistic theatre, which became a part of the essence of the West End. That meant that actors were happy to work in the smaller venues for less than their usual salaries, for their cause there was purely 'art'.

The West End remained however, whether for reasons of art or glamour, a lodestar through the thirties for almost everyone engaged in the drama. Sir John Gielgud says that, 'For a long time,' his ambition was, 'to be frightfully smart and West End, wear beautifully cut suits lounging on sofas in french window comedies.'[*11*] And even Tyrone Guthrie, whose successes had been in the most prestigious of art houses, was pleased when Binkie Beaumont invited him to produce in the West End in the thirties, for 'without at least some success in this sphere no one is regarded as fully professional.'[*12*] Although it seemed

130

anachronistic, as the nation drifted through recession to war, the West End sought above all to retain its smartness and glamour, the Edwardian graces which established its rank, and, as an inevitable product of both, its indelible narcissism.

Sir Noel Coward (right) learned 'everything he knew' from the leading figure of the Edwardian West End. Sir Charles Hawtrey (left).

10
The Rank and Snobbery of Sir Noel Coward

I have a Ritz mind and always have had. It is a genuine hangover from when I was really poor and had to endure bedbugs and cheap digs and squalor. I am unregenerate about this. To hell with local colour. I'd go mad if I spent one night in the ever so fascinating native quarter and that's that. *Noel Coward, Diary* 22nd April, 1960

From his first London success in 1924 with *The Vortex* to his final, admired appearance in 1966 in *Suite in Three Keys*, there is a sense in which one can say that for the twentieth century Noel Coward was the West End. He defined, through his public life and his inextinguishable commentary upon it, West End chic, just as the West End, in its turn, defined certain of his notions of professionalism.

Although he carefully assumed a persona that seemed smart and contemporary he was, in essential details, an Edwardian. One has to read very little of his writing before being struck by its jingoism. The simple and slightly emotional patriotism, the deep identification with Britain's causes in war and the benevolent amusement at most things foreign, were not characteristics of the majority of Britishers after 1914. And his formal grooming, with the immaculate dress, the polished manner, the high value put upon behaving 'beautifully' and, above all of those, the obsession with café 'society', were also characteristics of the pre-war smart set. Mainly however his behaviour in and around the theatre marked him most surely as Edwardian. The on-stage gestures, minimal, disciplined and deliberately theatrical, were more like those of Wyndham than like those of his contemporaries, and the languor and neo-Irving speech, clipped and nasal, together meant that he was more like Sir John Martin Harvey than, say, Sir Ralph Richardson. Off-stage his seemingly endless 'routs' and little dinners, at the homes of the Royal or fashionable, at the Savoy, the Ivy or the Ritz, recalled the socialising of the Edwardian actor managers, and when, finally, he began to acknowledge that he was perpetuating a style that had outlived its time, his reaction was one of anger at the apparent loss of Edwardian notions of rank and the intrusion of the general populace into what had been an exclusive arena. 'All elegance has fled from the West End,' he wrote in 1957, 'Coventry Street, Piccadilly Circus, Leicester Square and Shaftsbury Avenue have all acquired a curious 'Welfare State' squalor which reminds me of Moscow.' [1]

In content, although not in style, his diaries resemble those of Pepys. There is the same high value put upon the talk of the town, and the doings of the fashionable, and the theatre is often mentioned in a comparatively minor key, even when his own work was directly involved:

'The opening of *Lulu* at the New was a triumphant success and it's been playing to an average of £500 a performance ever since. I took Margot Fonteyn and Gina Lollobrigida and her husband. He was intelligent and amiable and she, I thought, was a trifle pleased with herself. She was also half an hour late. There was a pleasant party at Binkie's afterwards.

My other outings in London were *The Aspern Papers*, well done but a little dull; *The Hostage*, amateur, noisy and unattractive in every way; and a film, *I'm All Right, Jack*, which was brilliantly funny. Peter Sellers was superb, so really was everybody in it.

I dined with Binkie on my last evening and he was at his nicest and we heart-to-hearted until 3 a.m., by which time my friend was pissed as a newt.' [2]

The association with 'Binkie' Beaumont, who rose in the thirties to become first the joint managing director of the leading West End production management, H. M. Tennent, then its sole leader, is central to Coward's importance. Beaumont was the directly managerial facet of the West End world that Coward led, translating the high style of their partnership into practicalities. Their friendship was close until the 1950s—Beaumont is mentioned 130 times in Coward's published diaries, as fellow dinner guest, theatrical plotter and partner in West End enterprises—and when it temporarily cooled (Beaumont had not wished to produce Coward's *Waiting In The Wings*), Coward wrote as if their social relationship had constituted the essence of theatre, and as

134

if Beaumont's cooling friendship to him were synonymous with a fading love for the true drama. 'In the old days,' he wrote in 1960, '(Binkie) used to love the theatre and allow himself to be gently advised by John G, me, Joycie, etc.—now his advisers are John Perry, Prince Littler and Irene Selznick, and the change is *not* for the better.' [3]

During his temporary disillusionment with Beaumont, Coward accused him of becoming too interested in money. Such a charge could not justly have been levelled against Coward himself, although late in his professional life a huge overdraft forced him into re-ordering his life so he could survive comfortably into old age. Normally however the rank of society in which he dined was of far more concern to him than the size of the bill, and, when he had decided not to sign up for a television interview series in 1959, which would have paid him a total of £120,000, he remarked that he had drawn back from earning such sums because the people concerned with it were all 'ineradicably common', adding, 'I've seldom, no *never* in my life done anything only for money.' [4]

The rank of society in which Coward moved was extraordinary. His factotum and friend, Cole Lesley, records his awe, when he went to work for him in 1936, at the 'theatrically, socially and politically famous' who came to the studio from which Coward conducted his affairs, and at Coward's nonchalance in such company:

> 'Lady Cunard rang to ask if Mr Coward would come on Thursday after the theatre; she was having a quiet supper for the King. A thrilling message to pass on, I thought, but Noel shouted, 'I am sick to DEATH of having quiet suppers with the King, AND Mrs Simpson. Tell her I can't.' [5]

He was an intimate of many of the Royal Family, but in particular Lord Mountbatten and the Queen Mother. He dined with Prime Ministers; during the war he knew Robert Menzies well, and was on terms of some familiarity with Churchill, 'receiving him' in his box (9th October 1941) at the height of the war, and staying with the Prime Minister at Chequers in conditions of some intimacy:

> 'Woke after a practically sleepless night, with a heaviness on my mind. Talked to the PM, who was sitting up in bed. He thanked me really touchingly for all I had been doing for the troops.' [6]

Such intimacy with persons of the highest rank led him to pass patrician judgements upon them. After dining with Eden and his wife at the Perroquet in 1943 he solemnly announced that Anthony Eden was not 'quite up to being a Prime Minister yet.' It led him to assume that his position as West End star quite naturally placed him at the heart of the nation's affairs:

'Dined with Juliet (Duff). Just her, the Prime Minister and me. A lovely evening. He was at his most benign and suddenly, at the same moment, we both became emotional about him. He was immensely touched and simple about it. It was a strange but, I suppose, a very natural moment.' [7]

To some it would of course not seem natural at all, still less *very* natural, that an unlettered actor should emotionally patronise Britain's Prime Minister.

He viewed the working classes distantly, and with a certain revulsion. He disliked the 'obvious regimentation' of the Welfare State and accused it both of enforcing rigid behaviour, and of permitting too much lassitude. He was convinced that if ordinary people did not pull out of their apathy the country had no future:

'I have a core of sadness about England, sadness mixed with a sort of desolate irritation that a country and people so rich in tradition and achievements should betray itself and what it stands for by so whole-heartedly submitting to foolish government, natural laziness, woolly thinking and, above all, the new religion of mediocrity. The age of the common man has taken over a nation which owes its very existence to uncommon men.' [8]

By contrast however he had a high regard for West End audiences, whom he chose to see as intelligent and discriminating. The diaries are full of entries rejoicing in the fact that although his work was frequently reviled by the London critics, audiences still came to Coward plays.

It was however a particular segment of the general audience whose approval he sought. He was not a populist. He wrote in 1954:

'I have quite definitely decided not to do a season at the Palladium. Much as I love the theatre and the efficiency and niceness of all concerned, its not really my ambience. I could hold them all right for a quarter of an hour or even twenty minutes but not forty-five minutes. Oh no. Me for the more intimate lark to my own type of audience.' [9]

And he had moments of doubt over what he saw as the declining standards even of his own type of West End audience. Certainly he recoiled from the standards of the larger London audience, and even from the West End following of others.

This is shown most clearly in his relationship with Ivor Novello who,

136

briefly, shared the mantle of West End leader with him. In some respects Novello inhabited a world similar to Coward's—a well-groomed, consciously 'smart', predominately homosexual world of West End intrigue and high-living. Like Coward, Novello had contacts with, and the approval of, the Royal family. But there was a common touch about Novello which Coward disliked. W. Macqueen-Pope (who was Novello's publicity agent) puts it with uncharacteristic straightforwardness:

'So I shall not tell you of that social life of his, a very small and circumscribed one. He never went into 'Society' as do so many theatrical people today, for he did not like it and was more at home with folk of his own origin.' [10]

Novello's populist leanings—'Vulgarity' in Coward's parlance—brought him at times into opposition with Coward. Cole Lesley recounts one such encounter:

'Noel admired the lovely melodies that flowed from Ivor with no apparent effort; his admiration was less unbounded when it came to Ivor's straight comedies and the books of his musicals. They were honest with each other about such matters, and on two occasions—Ivor's *Downhill* and *The Rat*—Noel was called in by anxious friends, Constance Collier and Sir Gerald du Maurier, to deal with the grave situation. There were very serious talks indeed over luncheon at the Ivy about Ivor's terrible new play: 'You must deal with it, you are the only one he will listen to. We must all go down to Brighton and you will see for yourself; it is too ghastly for words, we cannot allow him to bring it in. You must stop him.' Noel did as he was bid and told Ivor the uncompromising truth, to which he appeared to listen gratefully, then did exactly what he had planned to do all along: open in the West End where the plays ran for many months to audiences packed with Ivor's adoring fans.' [11]

Novello's audience was different from Coward's, as his social life was differently based. For Coward, distinguished company invariably meant that he enjoyed his boredom, but the distinguished company was neither from his family nor from his profession. When he was fifty nine he wrote:

'In private I suppose I am a tremendous celebrity snob, and by celebrity I don't mean Brigitte Bardot but people of achievement like Somerset Maugham or Rebecca West. Looking back through my life I find that my personality only really changed once, and that

137

was when I was twenty four and I became a star and a privileged person.

. . . Looking around me I deplore the lack of style and elegance in most modern plays; I long for the glamour of the great stars who used to drive up to the stage door in huge limousines.' [12]

The nostalgia for a passing West End world is characteristic of the later Coward, but the significant thing is that his 'style and elegance' continued, up to 1960, to find its own 'distinguished company' to respond to it. In the fifties, when the Royal Court theatre supposedly had spearheaded a 'revolution' in British theatre, replacing for once and for all the drawing room trivia of the society drama with the kitchen-sink realism of the radicalised theatre, Coward's work continued to find and to please its West End audience. *Look After Lulu* (1959) and *Waiting In The Wings* (1960), although produced after the revolution of the mid-fifties, gained audiences equally large as those for *Relative Values* (1951), *Quadrille* (1952) and *Nude With Violin* (1956).

It is significant too that in any discussion of Coward's importance, as in discussion of the West End itself, we soon retreat from discussing the art, and turn to a discussion of the total ambience. In the words of the dramatic critic Kenneth Tynan, writing in 1953:

'He is perfectly well aware that he possesses 'star quality', which is the lodestar of his life. In his case it might be defined as the ability to project, without effort, the outline of a unique personality, which had never existed before him, in print or paint.

Even the youngest of us will know, in fifty years' time exactly what we mean by 'a very Noel Coward sort of person.' (*13*]

11
The Interval of the War

Dame Maud   **Oh, I didn't know it was social purpose**
                that brought us here. I thought it was
                C.E.M.A.
Edna   **C.E.M.A. is social purpose.**
Dame Maud   **Is it dear? Fancy!**

Terence Rattigan, Harlequinade   1948

War was announced on 3rd September 1939. In London the professional theatre was thrown into immediate disarray. Although it was not elsewhere unexpected—indeed 43% of the population interviewed on the 1st September had said they thought it was best to have a war and get it over with [*1*] — managers reacted with something approaching panic. Most London theatres, like the fledgling television service, closed immediately, and, as had happened in the first World War, this was followed somewhat limply by an official 'order' that cinemas and theatres should shut for the duration. There followed a sequence of events remarkably like those of 1914. Objections to closure were given succinctly by G.B. Shaw in a letter to *The Times:*

> 'May I be allowed to protest vehemently against the order to close all theatres and picture-houses during the war? It seems to me a masterstroke of unimaginative stupidity. During the last war we had 80,000 soldiers on leave to amuse every night. There were not enough theatres for them and rents rose to fabulous figures. Are there to be no theatres for them this time? . . . All actors, variety artists, musicians and entertainers of all sorts should be exempted from every form of service except their own all-important professional one.' [*2*]

As in the first World War a series of organisations for the dissemination of entertainment and the arts to troops and factory workers were formed during the first months. Amongst them were groups touring fit-up play productions such as M.E.S.A. (Mobile

139

Entertainments for the Southern Area), and later the play unit of A.B.C.A. (Army Bureau of Current Affairs). A small organisation set up by money from the Pilgrim Trust called C.E.M.A. (Council for the Encouragement of Music and the Arts) was concerned initially with the encouragement of amateurs, but abruptly changed its policy in the middle of 1940, promoted professional work, and became the genesis of the post-war Arts Council. Much larger and more significant in terms of wartime entertainment and drama was E.N.S.A. (Entertainments National Service Association, an organisation run by Basil Dean—organised in rather the same spirit as the Garrison Theatres run by the 1914-18 Canteen Committee—and which by the war's finish had cost £14,000,000, played to 500,000,000 people and had employed, it is estimated, four out of five British actors at some time during hostilities. In the first weeks of the war, when all London theatres were closed, the E.N.S.A. organisation occupied the Drury Lane theatre, using dressing rooms as offices, the Board Room as a conference room, and the hallowed stage for rehearsals and for the auditioning of about a third of the 50,000 would-be performers who applied to be taken on. E.N.S.A. also appointed the indefatigable West End apologist W. Macqueen-Pope as publicity officer and, by the end of its first month in existence, it had staged 500 presentations of various kinds—variety bills, plays and illustrated lectures.

In its second month it staged nearly a thousand, but the majority were out of London, or in its suburbs. The city centre was blacked out and deserted in the evenings, and although the first E.N.S.A. production, Frank Harvey's *Saloon Bar*, commenced touring in October 1939 and actually played continuously on tour for three years, it never occupied a West End theatre. There was indeed, in the early months of war, considerable mutual suspicion between E.N.S.A. and the West End managers, although when some West End theatres did subsequently reopen an arrangement was made under the auspices of E.N.S.A. by which productions could, at the end of their West End runs, tour camp sites, factory stages and Garrison theatres.

It would be true to say that although some West End theatres reopened quite quickly—Noel Coward's *Design for Living*, starring Rex Harrison and Diana Wynyard, played in the West End in January 1940—the essential West End experience was absent for the duration. The closure of restaurants, the difficulty of maintaining private transport or of finding adequate public services late at night, the sudden disappearance of elegant clothing, all meant that the high living and sense of chic associated with visiting the stalls of a pre-war West End theatre were impossible to stimulate. The fear of night raids meant in any case that many theatres played matinees only, or gave performances that started at six o'clock. In the circumstances it was hardly a mark of changing attitudes, but only a sign of the shortages of war that evening dress—for long an outward and visible sign of the West End's impeccable burgeois respectability—disappeared from the stalls and dress circle.

More important things however disappeared during the Battle of Britain, which began on 13th August 1940, and which led to the destruction of great tracts of the city. During the battle 12,000 tons of bombs were dropped on London, and 29,890 people were killed. It culminated in the most horrendous evening of all, the blitz of 10th May 1941, during which 2,200 fires were recorded in London, and 1,436 people died. In those nine months most theatres had closed again for a period—the exception in central London being the small Windmill theatre off Piccadilly which continued to offer its 'revues' of songs, comedy and nude posing in 'continuous performance' throughout the blitz. Many other theatres were damaged, including the Royal Court (which did not reopen until 1952), Duke of York's, Old Vic, Kingsway, Embassy and Sadler's Wells. Three theatre buildings were damaged beyond repair—the Shaftesbury, Little and Queens. In spite of the early performances audiences were frequently trapped in a theatre by an air raid warning during the day, and then they stayed within the theatre building, sometimes being given makeshift entertainment by the similarly trapped actors, and sometimes taking refuge in the subterranean parts of the theatre building alongside theatre staff and performers.

In the chaotic circumstances of war, when the carefully nurtured social constraints of West End theatre-going were perforce removed, and when the rough and ready systems of marketing and booking for performances no longer acted as a social filter, it is interesting to examine the kind of drama that found an immediate audience, and interesting to examine the means by which it did so. For it is arguable that in such conditions we can gain a better indication of a genuine popular response than in peacetime when there is so much more obvious manipulation of the public 'taste'. Certainly it is true to say that the dramatic performances which sprang up in London at lunchtimes and at matinees were in general more innovative and of higher literary quality than were the worthy tours sent out by E.N.S.A. Audiences were found for a variety of lunchtime dramatic entertainments, scantily advertised, costing very little, but far from patronising. At Wyndham's Edith Evans gave daytime poetry recitals. Donald Wolfit gave lunchtime Shakespearean recitals, initially at the Strand theatre. Most demanding of all, at the Westminster theatre, the literary scholar G. Wilson Knight, gave in 1941 a lecture/performance each lunchtime entitled *This Sceptered Isle*, a complex argument, based on the Shakespeare canon, about the nature of kingship and sovereignty in Britain. It played to packed audiences.

In management terms, the early months of the war offered release from the expensive and time-consuming rituals that had been associated with marketing and running West End shows. As Londoners read newspapers and listened to the radio more keenly than ever before they could now be easily and quickly notified of a new production. Shows could be much more cheaply mounted—acted by performers who asked for little in the way of salary, stage managed by skeletal crews who dropped for the duration the restrictive practices and demarcation lines of peacetime work. Plays were staged minimally, and, as drink and food were rationed or in short supply, theatres needed few sales staff. In such conditions the small venues, in particular the pre-war 'art' theatres, felt themselves to be competing on equal terms with their West End counterparts, and flourished accordingly. Used in any case to operating on low budgets, and without the expensive social trappings of their former rivals, they were able to find large audiences for work that would probably not otherwise have been seen in London. On occasion this was because some of the Little Theatres, being clubs, were able to give performances of plays which were not licensed by the censor—but in many cases it was simply that small theatre managements were better equipped to know that a modestly-sized market existed for serious work that was far from 'West End'. Of those small theatres that survived the blitz (casualties included the Gate, Neighbourhood, Torch and Threshold theatres), the Mercury presented classic repertory, including Congreve and Ibsen, and the Q theatre presented new writing. Most impressive was Unity theatre. It had started its life in a disused church hall in King's Cross in 1936, rapidly built a membership of 2,000 for its private performances of (predominately) left-wing dramas. It moved to larger premises in 1937 in

Goldington Street, the rebuilding and adaptation being carried out by its own members. Thereafter membership rose more rapidly still. A number of leading actors—Paul Robeson among them—turned their backs on West End stardom to appear with a company that believed 'true art effectively and realistically presented in the theatre can help the people to move towards the betterment of society'. At the outbreak of war Unity was the leading 'alternative' theatre, and had, within forty eight hours, written and produced a contemporary satirical revue *Sandbag Follies*, which was against militarism. Although not in the city centre, it shared with the Windmill the achievement of continuous performances through the blitz, and a continuous rise in audience numbers and reputation, culminating in John Allen's production of Sean O'Casey's *The Star Turns Red*, which prompted James Agate to assert that 'The most vital theatre in London is to be experienced in a back-street theatre in King's Cross—Unity.'

For a period the small alternative theatres were as numerous as the larger West End venues, and much livelier. Young companies were formed and ran theatres like Herbert Marshall's Neighbourhood theatre or Peter Ustinov's Threshold—both bombed—on shoestring budgets, and with minimal equipment. Many companies were overtly political, including the two Hampstead theatres founded by expatriate Germans, the Lantern and the Free German. Some, such as the Jewish theatre in the Grand Palais, existed to promote a particular dramatic culture. Others still, such as the co-operative group that ran the Arts theatre, presented normal high-class London drama seasons, but without the apparatus of West End management. It would not however be fair to conclude that by contrast with the alternative theatre the West End managements were totally supine. There were serious and important productions brought forward by long-standing West End managements which were both worth doing and found audiences—not least the productions led by John Gielgud; his 1940 *The Tempest*, his performance in the title role of *King Lear* and his 1942 *Macbeth* chief amongst them.

It was the production of *Macbeth*, initially presented by H. M. Tennent in the provinces as a straightforward commercial venture in 1941, that made some kind of history by being the first 'West End' production to take a wartime subsidy. By this time C.E.M.A. had, following a sudden demand in *The Times* that it should no longer concern itself with amateur groups, started to subsidise professional

Hugh (Binkie) Beaumont.   photo: *Angus McBean*

theatre work. The companies it supported were those which, like Martin Browne's Pilgrim Players, or the Old Vic company, were either charitable trusts or non-profit-sharing companies. Such groups had the further advantage that, secured against the taint of commercialism by their constitutions, and blessed by C.E.M.A.'s approval, they paid no entertainments tax. Plainly H. M. Tennent was a money-making firm, and as things stood, could hardly consider itself an educational or charitable organisation. However, wanting to bring *Macbeth* into the West End, and wanting both to avoid the tax and to gain some subsidy, Binkie Beaumont, partner in H. M. Tennent, created a new non-profit-sharing educational company, with the connivance of C.E.M.A. officers, called Tennent Plays Limited. It was duly aided by C.E.M.A. and avoided paying tax. However both *Macbeth*, and the second production *Love for Love*, indicated that H.M. Tennent's charitable concerns for the artistic well-being of London were making embarrassingly large profits. Both, it was suggested, could in fact have been successful under ordinary commercial conditions. In fairness however it must be said that some of the profits went to finance further small scale tours, and some to back a season of new plays at the Lyric, Hammersmith—both ventures which might not have been undertaken in ordinary commercial situations.

There was of course a considerable outcry against the 'arrangement' which enabled a private company to take refuge in state support. But other companies were formed by rival managements in a similar form. In 1944 Bronson Albery formed Una Plays as an 'educational' subsidiary of Wyndham's, and in 1945 Sherek Players were founded by commercial producer Henry Sherek. All worked in broadly the same way. The non-commercial company used the premises and know-how of the parent commercial company, and merely repaid a 'loan' from the parent company without interest, and, later, a modest weekly 'management fee'. The arrangement was, to put it mildly, open to abuse, but it had at least the merit that it helped to focus once more the long-established arguments within the theatre business about the ethics of state subsidy, and, always intermingled with those discussions, the desirability or otherwise of a National subsidised theatre.

The general opinion within West End managements at least had been that state interference could never be welcomed under any guise. The faithful mouthpiece Macqueen-Pope suggests the centrist attitude amongst the pre-war theatrical establishment towards such intrusions:

'The great peril of a National Theatre is that it will become a

Henry Sherek (right) was, like Sir Squire Bancroft (left), concerned with the refinement of West End taste.

146

museum, and not a theatre. It would, of course be run by a committee. The country being what it is, it is pretty safe to assert that the majority of that committee would be earnest, keen intelligent people, whose ideals and objects would be of the highest kind—but they would not be theatre people. That is the trouble.' [3]

What 'theatre people' were afraid of was that any state subvention in the theatre would inevitably run counter to the interests of the West End establishment.

To understand their fears it is necessary to recall that C.E.M.A.'s role in wartime had not remained constant. It had begun its operations as a kind of welfare agency, seeing the drama amongst other things as a means of general enlightenment and as a popular amateur activity. During the war it had changed and had operated in such a way as to promote professional theatre as a facet of national glory—the best maintained at its peak for the discriminating. There was however considerable anxiety lest any peacetime Arts Council should revert to a populist, welfare, stance, and a National Theatre might be run of dissimilar lines from the West End. It is this which causes Macqueen-Pope, revealingly, to say that the top theatre people did *not* share 'ideals and objects of the highest kind' with state planners. Their fear was that the post-war national Arts Council might be a part of a new Welfare State, with a concern for the entirety of the population, and such notions were of course antithetical to those of the West End establishment.

The West End retained in the post-war years only a little of its former "glamour". Stage door Johnnies were now dressed in utility clothing.

12
The West End in the Welfare State

I would not say that Mr. Hugh Beaumont, the shrewd, attractive and amusing head of the Tennent combine is a Jeckyll and Hyde, nor even a Box and Cox. As the No. 1 magnate of the London theatre, he has been seduced by the pranks of the Treasury to assume a dual personality. The Arts Council willed it so, and he has accepted the decree.

Young Mr. Beaumont, soft-voiced, modest and stage struck, saw himself becoming a semi-reluctant czar. He did not want to be dictator. He only wished to be in a position to dictate.

Beverley Baxter, *The Tale Behind a Top Talent Line-Up* 1953

In the forties Britain became a Welfare State, marked particularly by the passing of the *1944 Education Act*, which, amongst other things, created a compulsory system of state secondary education, and by the passing of the *1946 National Health Service Act* which, when it finally became operational in July 1948, gave Britain a comprehensive system of health care. Such momentous acts of general welfare were however carried out in spite of the prevailing economic conditions rather than because of them. The country could ill afford the new expenditure. The war debt had risen until by the end of the war we were losing £14,000,000 a day, with the result that we owed the United States, who had given aid to prop up the economy, a sum in excess of £10,000,000,000. For most people the basic commodities were scarce—clothing, flour, eggs, soap and milk were not de-rationed until 1950. Demobilised servicemen returned to bombed cities, linked by worn-out railways and unreliable bus services, and they took boring jobs in Britain's antiquated factories, for which the average wage was £6 a week.

Cold, poorly-stocked and overcrowded homes were not, in spite of the continuing popularity of the B.B.C. radio service, the places in which the majority wished to spend all their leisure time. Radio drama had a huge post-war audience—30% of the entire population listened to *Saturday Night Theatre* and *Appointment With Fear*—but there was a vast and ready market, as there had been following the *1843 Theatres Act*, for the large-scale public spectaculars. The cinema was hugely popular—its takings rose from £50,000,000 in 1945 to £108,000,000 by 1950, and in the peak year of 1948 it had 1,514,000,000 attendances. In that same year 41,000,000 spectators watched professional soccer which, like all sport, enjoyed a post-war boom in attendances. At Olympia each year the Bertram Mills organisation presented their circus, new management practices creating a beautifully marketed and presented show that was not only the best in Europe, but was so successful that a substantial number of seats in the 5,000-seater complex were sold for the *following* year during each lengthy Christmas season[1]. Thus in spite of the post-war austerity, Britons spent freely on common amusements of all kinds—between 1945 and 1950 they spent more than £500,000,000 on dog racing and the pools, and in 1950 alone spent £766,000,000 on alcohol—and flocked in their hundreds of thousands to anything spectacular, colourful and entertaining.

The West End theatre was however not able to take part in the boom. Managements could not expand their theatre capacities, as sports administrators could easily expand *their* stadiums. The traditional expensive practices of production could not seemingly be altered, certainly not in the way circus practices were modified at Olympia by the Mills family. By 1947 London theatre was troubled further on two more immediate counts[2]. First, the population of central London, already declining, had been scattered by wartime bombing, and so it was a more difficult and expensive journey into the West End after the war than had been the case before. The government had succeeded by 1950 in building 806,000 new homes and 157,000 'temporary' prefabricated dwellings, but a tiny part of that was in city centres. In London even the new housing estates tended to be built very far from the centre, partly because of the establishment of the 'green belt' on which no housing could be erected[3]. Indeed a considerable part of London's displaced population left the capital altogether, and moved to one of the new towns on London's periphery. Ten years after the war each of these new towns—Basildon, Bracknell, Hemel Hempstead, Hatfield, Stevenage, Harlow and Crawley—was expanding at the rate of

9,000 houses a year [4]. A second reason for the uncertain prospects for the post-war London theatre was that, in comparison with ordinary popular pleasures, it was expensive, and this, with the expense of a journey, made it an unrealistic possibility for many people. Whereas you could do the football pools for 2d., buy a pint of beer for 10d., get into your neighbourhood cinema and see the best films for 1s., to get into the West End, the 'best' theatre, cost 3s. even for a moderate seat, and on top of that the transport costs, price of a programme, and the cost of refreshments during a long period away from home had to be considered. [5]

There was no concerted attempt to woo back the popular audience, nor indeed to change managerial style. Far from reaching out to encompass new people and new thinking, the inner coterie of West End management contracted during the last years of the war and the first years of the peace. It was during the war that Prince Littler began to buy up London theatres and by 1949 he directly owned 18 out of 42 active West End venues. Binkie Beaumont, Prince Littler and his brother Emile were in the post-war years key members of 'The Group', an unofficial consortium that controlled more than half of the West End, and maintained it, so far as was possible, in its Edwardian manner.

Anyone trying to break into management, from outside the charmed circle, found it extremely difficult. This was in part because the constant incestuous 'arrangements' and sub-letting of West End properties meant that to the outsider theatres were even more expensive. As Peter Daubeny said, 'Leases had changed hands a great many times, and, through this sub-letting, the rent charged to the producing manager had increased three or four times over.'[6] In part too it was because theatres were genuinely occupied; plays had, on average, three times the run of a pre-war West End production. But it was generally felt that the important factor was that the leaders of 'The Group', Prince Littler in particular, exercised an autocratic power. Daubeny remarked that the West End theatre was falling more and more into monopolistic control, and that, 'The chances of a new and original play ever seeing the light depends in a vast degree upon its meeting the taste of one particular person.'[7] Nor was the post-war power of West End management confined to the capital. As J. B. Priestley remarked:

> 'Even in these new days it is these managers who do more than anybody else to shape and colour the theatrical life of this country. Their successful productions not only occupy the chief London

151

playhouses for months and months and sometimes years on end, but they provide most of the plays for provincial tours and repertory companies and the amateurs. The new piece they describe with enthusiasm at the Ivy restaurant today will probably, within the next three years, be applauded from Torquay to Aberdeen.' [8]

Priestley went on to say, without equivocation, 'What I condemn is the property system which allows public amenities and a communal art to be controlled by persons rich enough to acquire playhouses.'[9] He wanted the theatre in some way to be in the hands of the profession.

The difficulty was that, for most practical purposes, 'The Group' *was* the profession. They owned the majority of the most important playhouses—the salons of the remaining West End audience—and influenced the livelihoods of actors unknown to them by having control of the only places in which the 10,000 members of post-war Equity could find recognition and a degree of job security[10]. Although the provinces were filled with a brief crop of fit-up weekly repertory companies the pay in them was dreadful, and the post-war television service had not then begun to offer another source of lucrative employment. Although a few actors led their own specialist companies, and a fewer number did so with success[11], the majority looked to the West End for inspiration still. Their dream was that of the hero of John Drummond's successful 1947 novel *Playing to the Gods*, who moved from touring in fifth-rate companies to 'West End successes and world fame.' [12]

The implication that the West End was automatically first-rate can be accepted in one sense only. The technical values of some West End productions—particularly those mounted by H. M. Tennent—were undoubtedly very high. The dramatic and literary values however, where they can be said to have existed at all, were anachronistic and limp. The theatre clung resolutely to its Edwardian world. The highest estimate suggests that there were fewer than 600 butlers working in post-war Britain,[13] but an observer who thought to learn anything of the timbre of post-war life from the West End theatre would have assumed there were hundreds of thousands, as few stage families seemed to be without one. They would have assumed too that no family lived without five guest bedrooms, a tennis court, vast gardens, and a retinue of under-servants. As Robert Hewison remarks:

'In one part of England the country house continued to flourish as though there had never been a war; on the London stage. The drawing room, with its telephone and french windows, was the almost permanent setting for a series of light romantic comedies, family melodramas and detective thrillers, of which Agatha Christie's *The Mousetrap*, first played in 1952 and still playing in 19(83), remains a venerable example.' [14]

More important than the merely anachronistic surroundings was the deadly, ingrown quality of theatrical dialogue, which was incapable for the most part of conveying anything that was not artificial, falsely-coloured and thin. The plays of the West End—given in Figure 9 for the year 1950—were plays in which, to quote Kenneth Tynan's contemporary observation, 'Joys and sorrows are giggles and whimpers: the crash of denunciation dwindles into 'Oh, stuff, Mummy!' and 'Oh, really, Daddy!' And so grim is the continuity of these things that the foregoing might have been written at any time during the last thirty years.' [15]

As far as was possible the West End establishment contrived to recreate the social niceties of the years before the first, rather than the second, World War. Curtain-up moved back to 7.15 p.m. so that the theatre could once more be an after-dinner relaxation, and the stalls again tried to reflect some of the elegance that was presented on stage. It became once more the fashion to 'dress' for first nights, and a considerable section of the West End audience would have liked to go further. Beverley Baxter wrote in the *Evening Standard* in 1954:

'Unless it is a first night there will hardly be a dinner jacket or a tails to be seen unless it is the manager having a look. If it were a Masonic dinner or a Chamber of Commerce dinner and dance, or a Conservative Association Annual Dinner, everyone would be in evening dress . . .

Do not imagine it is the wife who wants to go 'just as we are'. No woman is too tired to put on a new dress. In fact they are like children in their dressing up. I must admit, however, that the hour of 7-15 makes this difficult (although not impossible).

Therefore let the theatres have the courage to return to the hour of 8 or 8-15. It is for the managements to play their part in restoring the glamour.' [16]

In the correspondence which followed there was vigorous support for Baxter. Mrs. Isabella H. Nicholson, of Kensington Square Gardens, pointed out that the lone Briton in the 'outposts of Empire' deemed it his duty to dress for dinner although there was no one to see him, and 'This effective gesture against boredom and slovenliness should be an

Figure 9

Plays Opening in the West End — 1950

Date	Play	Theatre	Revival	Contemporary	'Poetic Drama'	Revue	Comedy	Farce	Mystery	Problem Play	Musical	'Classic'
January												
17	**The Miser**	New	●				●					
18	**Venus Observed**	St. James		●	●							
26	**Ring Round the Moon**	Globe		●			●					
February												
1	**The Schoolmistress**	Saville	●				●					
2	**Hamlet**	New	●									●
7	**Larger Than Life**	Duke of York's	●							●		
March												
2	**The Way Things Go**	Phoenix		●			●					
7	**Home at Seven**	Wyndham's		●					●			
9	**Mr Gillie**	Garrick		●						●		
20	**Latin Quarter 1950**	Casino		●							●	
25	**Detective Story**	Princes		●						●		
April												
19	**The Green Bay Tree**	Playhouse	●							●		
27	**Sauce Piquante**	Cambridge		●		●						
May												
3	**The Cocktail Party**	New		●	●							
10	**The Holly and the Ivy**	Duchess		●						●		
18	**Background**	Westminster		●						●		
19	**Touch and Go**	Prince of Wales's		●			●					
23	**His Excellency**	Princes		●						●		
June												
7	**Carousel**	Drury Lane		●							●	
14	**Seagulls Over Sorrento**	Apollo		●			●					
15	**Golden City**	Adelphi		●							●	
28	**The Dish Ran Away**	Whitehall		●				●				
July												
7	**Ace of Clubs**	Cambridge		●							●	
19	**Mister Roberts**	Coliseum		●						●		

Date	Play	Theatre	Revival	Contemporary	'Poetic Drama'	Revue	Comedy	Farce	Mystery	Problem Play	Musical	'Classic'
August												
5	**Don't Lose Your Head**	Saville		●				●				
9	**Captain Carvallo**	St. James's		●			●					
22	**Rosmersholm**	St. Martin's	●									●
23	**The Little Hut**	Lyric		●			●					
29	**The Second Mrs Tanqueray**	Haymarket	●							●		
September												
4	**Spring Song**	Saville		●						●		
6	**Will Any Gentleman?**	Strand		●				●				
7	**Accolade**	Aldwych		●						●		
12	**Reluctant Heroes**	Whitehall		●				●				
October												
5	**Journey's End**	Westminster	●							●		
11	**Top of the Ladder**	St. James's		●						●		
12	**The Fourposter**	Ambassadors		●			●					
13	**Dear Miss Phoebe**	Phoenix		●								●
24	**Who is Sylvia?**	Criterion		●			●					
30	**Take It From Us**	Adelphi		●		●						
31	**Party Manners**	Princes		●			●					
November												
23	**To Dorothy, A Son**	Savoy		●			●					
December												
14	**Lace On Her Petticoat**	Ambassadors	●								●	

In 1950 H. M. Tennent Ltd. presented **Traveller's Joy** (Criterion), **Seagulls Over Sorrento** (Apollo), **Mister Roberts** (Coliseum), **Home At Seven** (Wyndham's), **Accolade** (Aldwych), **Who Is Sylvia?** (Criterion), **The Little Hut** (Lyric) in addition to the long running **Harvey** (Piccadilly).

Tennent Productions Ltd., in Association with the Arts Council of Great Britain, also presented in the West End **A Streetcar Named Desire** (Aldwych), **Treasure Hunt** (Apollo), **Ring Round the Moon** (Globe), **The Holly and the Ivy** (Duchess), **Treasure Hunt** (St. Martin's), **The Second Mrs Tanqueray** (Haymarket) and the production of **The Heiress** (Haymarket) which it replaced.

Tennent Productions also presented, at the Lyric Theatre, Hammersmith, **Shall We Join the Ladies?** and **The Boy With A Cart, Man of the World, If This Be Error, The Beggar's Opera, View Over The Park, The Old Ladies, Point of Departure, Let's Make An Opera** and **Tartuffe.** As they were also presenting **Oklahoma** at the Stoll theatre, this list of 16 West End and 10 'non-commercial' productions gives an indication of the extent of Tennent's dominance of London theatrical production.

example to the 'don't care' attitude of many today.' Duncan Grant, of Westbourne Park Villas, urged that West End shows should begin at 8-30. Rufus J. Harris, of Greencroft Gardens, asked plaintively 'Must we leave it to the 'Edwardians' to give the touch of elegance and dash with which a high-spirited people graces its hours of leisure?' Not everyone however saw it as the West End manager's job to restore that kind of glamour, and R. K. Martin of Loughborough saw Baxter's views as dangerous, taking the theatre back to the 'theatrically dismal days when the audience glittered and the shows stank.' [17]

The managers did not take any action to enforce compulsory formality of dress, but as the austerity eased the West End audiences themselves began to bring back some of the former glamour. By 1950 the newsworthy were once more being photographed at first nights wearing what was fashionable. In the theatre foyers a board would announce the time the show ended so that cars—there were 2,250,000 private cars in Britain in 1950—could collect the privileged from what had been, too often, boredom spent in distinguished company, or, to quote the somewhat more earthy tag of Mr Martin, a stinking show played to a glittering audience. 'The bare fact is,' said Kenneth Tynan in 1954, 'that, apart from revivals and imports, there is nothing in the London theatre that one dares discuss with an intelligent man for more than five minutes.' [18]

The situation should of course have been of great concern to the new post-war Arts Council of Great Britain which, formed from the administrative framework of the wartime Council for the Encouragement of Music and the Arts, had received its first Royal Charter in 1946[19]. Its first object was to improve the practice of the arts, and it might be thought that, even though its financial resources were not large, it would have turned its back upon the curious mausoleum that, for the post-war decade, the West End theatre had become. Yet, for a part of that time at least, there was a strange partnership between the Arts Council and 'The Group'—the one ostensibly interested in the promotion of the best drama, the other interested in the maintenance of expensive social rituals which ran counter to the promotion of anything other than the well-made, well-dressed West End vehicle—and they made common cause.

To conceive of this strange partnership one has to understand a little more about the Arts Council. Although it was chartered at the same time as the country was creating great agencies of social welfare, its own roots lay elsewhere. One can say, in the broadest terms, that a national arts council that dispenses money may seek to do so with either of two objectives. It may seek above all to sustain the national art heritage, that approved emblematic art by which a nation's character is supposed to be known and which—in national galleries, in national opera houses and on national theatre stages—is understood and approved by the influential and privileged. We may then say that it is operating according to a *Glory Model*. The alternative objective we can term the *Welfare Model*. An arts council will then seek to stimulate all arts equally, to use them as an agency of general enlightenment and welfare, and to encourage the artist to see himself as servant of some tangible social ideal. Our own Arts Council plainly had its roots in the patrician attitudes of Lord Keynes and his set, the pre-war 'Apostles' who 'enjoyed supreme self confidence, superiority and contempt towards all the rest of the unconverted world.' [20] It could not conceivably have tolerated working with 'The Group' had it aspired to the Welfare notion of arts provision; that it was able to work with 'The Group' is because, in spite of a certain rhetorical blurring of its purposes, the post-war Arts Council actually worked according to the Glory model.

As Lord Drogheda has revealingly explained in his 1978 memoirs *Double Harness*, an important 'understanding' was reached in 1946 between the chairman of the Covent Garden board, Sir John Anderson, and the Chancellor of the Exchequer of the day, Hugh Dalton, in the form of a pledge by the government to the national opera house:

'The somewhat vague wording of the pledge was to the effect that if Covent Garden played its part the Government (through the size of its grant to the Arts Council: J.P.) would not let Covent Garden down; and, like a good public servant he held it to be morally binding on all future Chancellors until formally withdrawn or annulled.' [21]

In other words, the government grant to the Arts Council was, without formal contract but with the considerable force of a gentleman's agreement, always to be conditional upon them supporting, above all, the Royal Opera House at Covent Garden. So large and so central a commitment to Glory meant that, even if the instincts of the founding fathers of the Arts Council had inclined them in that direction they *could* not have operated according to the Welfare Model in their support of theatre. They were, in effect, forced to act as persons of the highest rank and, as such, had purposes in common with the West End establishment. Although some observers were worried by the wider implications of the relationship, the Drama Officers of the new Arts

1st August, 1946.

This is in reply to your letter of the 26th July,
in which you ask me to review my attitude to the Covent
Garden Trust as expressed in my letter to Pooley of the
15th July.

The assistance which the Covent Garden Trust
receives from the Exchequer will, of course, come to it
through the Arts Council. You will understand that in
general I should wish the Council to feel themselves
responsible for the allocation of the funds which
Parliament puts at their disposal, and to plan their
work ahead in the expectation of an assured but limited
grant.

I recognise, however, that the magnitude of the
Covent Garden undertaking and the difficulty in present
circumstances of estimating its future needs places it
in a special position, and that the State will be assuming
a definite obligation to see to it that, subject to others
playing their part, Opera is not let down. I do not
therefore rule out the possibility that the fulfilment
of this obligation might in certain circumstances make it
necessary to increase the Treasury grant to the Arts
Council still further than I undertook in my letter of
the 15th July. It would, I think, be agreed that these
circumstances would not be held to have arisen unless in
any year the Trust could show a need for a grant from the
Arts Council of an amount exceeding £60,000.

I am sending a copy of this letter to Pooley.

(Sgd.) HUGH DALTON.

The Rt. Hon. Sir John Anderson, G.C.B., G.C.S.I.

*The Chancellor's letter to Sir John Anderson is the only outward sign
that Government funding to the Arts Council is given on the understanding that, whatever happens, 'Opera is not let down'.*

Council and 'The Group' began to move in the same world. The wartime support of C.E.M.A. for the non-profit-making Tennent Plays Limited was continued into peacetime by the Arts Council. There was a good deal of socialising in the clubs, and each sought 'advice' from the other. By 1949/50 the composition of the Arts Council Drama Panel betrays a heavy West End influence. It was:

Sir Bronson Albery (Chairman)

Miss Peggy Ashcroft	John Gielgud
Mr John Burrell	E. A. Harding
Dame Edith Evans	Hugh Hunt
Andre Van Gyseghem	Laurence Olivier
Norman Higgins	Eric Landless Turner
Michael MacOwan	Hugh 'Binkie' Beaumont
Stephen Thomas	Noel Coward
Leslie Banks	Tyrone Guthrie
Lewis Casson	Patrick Henderson
Benn Levy	Willard Stoker

Enough of the names will already be known to the reader of this book to indicate how strongly the West End establishment was represented, and enough of them are known to hazard the guess that many regional interests, to say nothing of the interests of much other dramatic entertainment, were unrepresented.

The financial reverberations of this alliance were great. Producing managements that did not enjoy any kind of support from the Arts Council or from 'The Group' continued to pay the 1916 Entertainments Tax, and, if they found a theatre in London at all, paid inflated rentals to the lessees. Thus it was possible, according to an example given by Priestley, [22] for a show to arrive in London after a successful tour, £1,500 down on production costs and yet having paid the Treasury some £11,000 in Entertainment Tax. If it were successful in London its weekly profit was much diminished by the high theatre rental, and by the necessity of continuing to pay off the production costs. Even so, an eventual weekly 'profit' of £300 could well be wiped out by paying three times that sum in Tax. Yet the Arts Council chose to act as if those managements outside the group could take care of themselves. In 1946, during the first full year of their operation, the Council allocated only £45,510. 18s. 2d. to the national drama, some 18% of the total Government Grant of £255,000. By 1950 the sum allocated to the drama has risen to £119,016. 18s. 11d. which was roughly 19.5% of the total grant the Arts Council was given. But thereafter, through the fifties, the Council gave a decreasing percentage of its funds to the drama and, it might be said, left London's theatre (and, by extension, a considerable part of the national drama) largely in the hands of a coterie which aimed still for 'fastidious exclusiveness'.

	Total Arts Council Grant	Percentage Allocated to Drama
1950	£600,000	19.5 per cent.
1951	£675,000	14.0 per cent.
1952	£875,000*	11.5 per cent.
1953	£675,000	11.0 per cent.
1954	£785,000	9.0 per cent.
1955	£785,000	8.0 per cent.
1956	£820,000	8.0 per cent.
1957	£885,000	8.0 per cent.
1958	£985,000	7.5 per cent.
1959	£1,110,000	7.0 per cent.

* inflated by the inclusion of a final payment to the Council for its part in the Festival of Britain.

By contrast the allocations to music in 1957 and 1958 were £514,016. 3s. 11d. and £654,000. 11s. 10d. At the time Opera and Ballet were included in the general music figures, but those sums were respectively 58% and 66% of the total grant. In the sixties the percentage of the total grant allocated to drama steadily rose however. By 1965 around 17% of the total allocation went to drama, and by 1970 the figure was some 23%.

The abandonment of the national drama to 'The Group' was not of course total. 'Worthwhile' touring companies and some provincial repertory companies were aided, as in their turn were young people's theatre companies and the various phases of small-scale alternative theatre—but the huge monolith of the West End was not positively challenged. The uneasy partnership of the Council and the West End establishment was rarely—indeed, *is* rarely—discussed, and when either side mentioned it, there was a notable unease and, as happened when B. Ifor Evans and Mary Glasgow approached the liaison in *The Arts in England*, a tendency to fall back on platitude:

'It is an open question how much can be done by public authority, State control or State funds, to keep the theatre safe from abuse by private money-makers. The opposite abuse of regulation by government office lurks very near at hand, and Parliamentary safeguards are unfortunately all too often negative in action. The temptation to 'play safe' may prove even greater to the government agency than to the business syndicate. On the other hand, it would be tragic if government support were to mean support only for unworthy failures. All things considered, we would urge the country's leaders in the theatrical field, if they value the health of the theatre and hope for its better future, to encourage variety in enterprise. The public is notoriously incalculable in its reception of the plays offered to it, and only in variety and constant experiment can be formed the kind of success which breeds success and not simply long runs.' [23]

By 1949 it was already obvious that government support through the Arts Council did not necessarily result in 'unworthy failures'. The twelve non-commercial managements working in some form of co-operation with the Arts Council gave some things that were worthy, although there were inevitably, by dint of the new arrangements, no *financial* successes. Laurence Olivier had seen as a hopeful sign that some wartime companies did not need to take up their proffered guarantee against loss[24]. And Priestley, in company with others, had expressed the hope that subsidies would not be necessary in the theatre for very long. However state-aided groups began to budget in a way that made it inevitable that their state monies would be seen not as a fallback guarantee against loss, but as a grant, a part of income which meant that prices, for subsidised drama, could be fixed at a lower uncommercial level.

Again voicing a general sentiment Priestley had said that low theatre prices were a necessary part of a strategy to restore a popular theatre [25]. But after a decade of peace there were few indications that keeping prices low by subsidy was attracting a new audience, and in the mid-fifties a cynic would have been justified in saying that the only very obvious effect of state subsidy was to fossilise a theatre still dominated by the West End. The post-war revival of 'poetic drama' was petering out. Acting styles were, like styles of management, showing very little change—and the subsidy was more than anything subsidising the life-style of an ageing, already privileged audience. And it was, because it kept seat prices low, having a distinctly *adverse* effect upon the unaided, commercial theatre. Therefore it had the reverse effect from that which Priestley hoped.

In 1956 there was however a much-discussed theatrical 'revolution' in which (according to the version current for the following decade) the non-West End theatre revitalised the British drama. This revolution, often said to come from the English Stage Company (a company formed, incidentally by a playwright, Ronald Duncan, and a commercial impresario, Oscar Lewenstein), was variously cited as being a justification of state subsidy, the virtual death of the old West End, and a complete overthrow of a century of theatrical rank and privilege.

From our present distance it is of course possible to see that the effects of the 'revolution' were actually very slight. One play, Osborne's *Look Back In Anger* was—like Coward's *The Vortex* had been— a great post-war success. Income from its tours, its overseas productions and its transfer meant that the Royal Court theatre, which had housed the English Stage Company premiere, was able to earn some £8,505 in 1956/57 and change a probable deficit of £3,500 into a £5,000 profit. And so great was the profit in the following year, together with income from further work by Osborne, that the Royal Court benefitted to the tune of nearly £40,000—an income five times greater than their promised Arts Council grant. But this was an exception, not the rule in some general popular revival. Most productions at the Royal Court between 1956 and 1960 lost money, and most new works played to average attendances of less than 50%—and that in a theatre with only 407 seats. The subsidy to the English Stage Company might therefore be justified upon the grounds that it enabled some new writing to have a professional stage production, but it could not be justified on the grounds that it enabled much of that writing to find an audience, still less a substantial *new* audience.

And although the West End managements certainly housed several significant transfers from the Royal Court, and from Stratford East, that can hardly be characterised in retrospect as the West End establishment being threatened by subsidised revolution. It was in the interests of the West End managers to take in some plays for which they did not have to pay rehearsal costs, which had an established reputation and for which there was already a known audience. Such transfers indeed were often more in the interests of the West End establishment than of the 'revolutionary' theatres; the work at Stratford East, in particular, suffered through transfer, for on each occasion the director had to start again with a relatively new company to build up the singular house style, a long, exhausting and relatively expensive procedure for which the income from a successful transfer did not always compensate.

Indeed a disinterested examination of the London theatre in the late fifties tends to show that, rather against the press comment at the time, the impact of the new plays produced in the West End upon the provincial and subsidised theatre was greater than the impact of the 'revolutionary' theatres upon the West End. It was after all West End impresario Donald Albery who first presented *Waiting for Godot* to British audiences. It was Michael Codron, a newcomer to West End management in the fifties, who first presented Harold Pinter's *The Birthday Party* in London, and who later gave the first London showings of work by Orton, Livings, Mortimer, Saunders and Halliwell. It was Oscar Lewenstein, who began his career in West End management in 1955, who presented *The Threepenny Opera* in London, and also gave showings to the work of Mankowitz and Arden. These plays and these authors were taken up by the so-called 'non-commercial' theatre after the event. An examination of work presented in the West End in one year, 1960, yields several plays that were given productions in subsidised venues after their 'commercial' productions—among them Michael Redgrave's version of Henry James' *The Aspern Papers* (first performed at the Queen's), Greene's *The Complaisant Lover* (Globe), Mortimer's *The Wrong Side of the Park* (Cambridge), Lawrence and Lee's *Inherit the Wind* (St. Martin's), Santha Rama Reu's adaptation of Forster's *A Passage to India* (Comedy), Jerome Kitty's *Dear Liar* (Criterion), Duerrenmatt's *The Visit* (Royalty), Bolt's *A Man for All Seasons* (Globe) and his other piece *The Tiger and the Horse* (Queen's).

Such a list helps to refute the notion that the West End was under siege from an outside threat. It also gives a clue to the fact that the revolution was in the well-made play's content, rather than its form. Almost all the plays above, *Look Back In Anger* amongst them, were presented as well-made, neatly-finished proscenium arch pieces to well-behaved properly-distanced audiences—with only their allusions to a fashionable notion of modernity to distinguish them. ('Kitchen sink' was the term for the new realism as 'cup and saucer' had been the epithet used a century earlier to describe the realism of T.W. Robertson). For the new audiences of the late fifties—'new' in that they now included some of the relatively affluent and highly educated post-war youngsters who were first generation members of the middle class—behaved in the theatre exactly as the docile audiences had done in the West End for a century or more. Their less privileged fellows rioted in cinemas during the showing of *Rock Around The Clock* but upon those who joined the live theatre audience the past sat contentedly.

Indeed it would be true to say that by 1960 it was apparent that the influence of the Bancrofts in the West End was still greater than any influence of the kitchen sink dramatists. In 80 years little changed in actual theatre management, and the difference between the West End and the growing subsidised sector of theatre did not lie in the nature of their programmes, their managerial aims, nor their managerial efficiency. Plays were marketed in much the same ways. The post-war subsidised theatres found and concentrated upon their own audiences, as the West End establishment concentrated upon theirs. When it suited them West End producing managements presented repertory seasons, and when it suited *them* the subsidised theatres bought in their 'stars'. The one clear difference was in seat pricing and after 1960 it was to be an increasing complaint of the unsubsidised managements that state subsidy enabled the subsidised theatres to present work to the public at lower prices, and so distort their traditional market. On every other issue there was surprising agreement, and although the post-war liaison between the Arts Council and 'The Group' had officially ceased in the fifties, there was still a general agreement that British theatre was in essence a pyramid, with, at its apex, that kind of expensive ritual that was still termed, and still sometimes with approval, *West End.*

13
The City and the Finale

Joy, energy and intelligence: these are the three
fundamental requisites of a people's theatre. This is but
an indication of the wholly new theatre which is possible
- a theatre that would really belong to our century.

Romain Rolland

Between 1945 and 1960 there were several serious attempts to recreate
a popular theatre by moving outside the confines of professional theatre
practice altogether. A first significant move was the formation, in May
1946, of the Little Theatre Guild of Great Britain, which brought
together a number of leading amateur companies who controlled their
own theatres—the Bradford Civic Theatre, the Newcastle People's
Theatre and the London Questors Theatre among them. Members did
not however look for new theatrical styles so much as look for high
standards in the performance of old ones, and the growth of the
movement was slow—by 1960 there were fewer than thirty members.
In the event it did not seem to represent a popular revival, and the
general pessimism of George Taylor seemed to be still justified:

> 'The Restoration Theatres linked the stage more closely with the
> Court and high society and by drawing its audiences from the
> fashionable classes, divorced it from the common people and made
> it the minority interest it has been ever since. That is until the
> growth of the amateur theatre in the twentieth century led people
> to believe that the theatre was at last being brought back to the
> people. From the way in which amateur groups came into being,
> one might accept this general statement as true. It is only when one
> attends B.T.A. and N.O.D.A. conferences and those of smaller
> organisations, set up to help the amateur theatre, that one realises
> how exclusive they are. Delegates in the main are drawn from the
> middle and professional classes and working-class representation
> is thin on the ground.' [1]

165

Figure 10

Duration of Daily Television Viewing 1955

Proportion of 12,040,000 members of the 'television audience' viewing:

	SUN	MON	TUES	WED	THURS	FRI	SAT
Viewing at all	81.2%	73.6%	75.2%	69.7%	61.5%	76.8%	69.7%
Up to 1 hour	15.1%	19.4%	19.6%	20.6%	24.6%	20.9%	11.8%
From 1 to 2 hours	18.6%	22.3%	24.6%	21.8%	19.8%	24.8%	16.3%
From 2 to 3 hours	30.9%	23.8%	22.1%	22.5%	12.8%	25.2%	27.6%
From 3 to 4 hours	14.5%	6.5%	7.8%	4.4%	2.9%	5.2%	11.1%
From 4 to 5 hours	1.6%	1.6%	0.9%	0.4%	1.1%	0.5%	2.6%
5 hours and over	0.5%	—	0.2%	—	0.3%	0.2%	0.3%
Not viewing	18.8%	26.4%	24.8%	30.3%	38.5%	23.2%	30.3%

Less hidebound was the Theatre in Education movement, which flourished in the years after the war, and whose history was recorded in the bulletin *Theatre in Education*, which was first published in 1947. Both its aims and methods were broad. It encompassed activities with young people that ranged from the self-expressive—particularly work inspired by the Educational Drama Association, founded by Peter Slade in 1943—to young people's theatre performances, such as those given by the touring Children's Theatre run by John Allen. It continued to grow through the fifties. The British Drama League formed its Junior Drama League in 1955, which led to a national residential school for young people in 1958. And in 1956 Michael Croft formed the National Youth Theatre, which drew its young actors from all over the country and which played an annual season in a London theatre.

In one sense the success of ventures such as Michael Croft's signalled the limitations of the post-war boom in young people's theatre. For, in order to establish its status, the National Youth Theatre had to play to critics and audiences that were all-but West End, and even presented young actors who, depressingly, aped the limp reflexes and high style of the West End performer. In the late fifties there were already signs that the movement to promote drama as an educational activity for young people, which had led drama to be a new main subject in teacher's training colleges and a separate subject in school curricula, was itself also limited by its flirtation with the establishment theatre. Thus College courses in dramatic improvisation and techniques of popular drama would too often end up by presenting, as their major activity, well-thumbed, well-made plays. It was significant too that when the movement for young drama had so permeated higher education that the *Sunday Times* felt it expedient to back the National Student Drama Festival—an annual event begun in 1955—it was that newspaper's professional critic, Harold Hobson, who set the seal upon the Festival's standards by judging the winner of the Sunday Times Trophy. So it was scarcely surprising when, in 1966, the impresario Peter Bridge actually presented the winning play in the West End itself, and the world of student drama was thus seen in its entirety to be what the Cambridge Footlights and the Oxford University Dramatic Society had long been, tributaries of the West End theatre rivalling the specialist drama colleges.

By the mid-fifties both radio and the cinema were fast losing their popularity. Indeed the cinema's attendances fell spectacularly, and in 1960 the annual admissions, 500,800,000, were less than half the admissions in 1950, 1,395,800,000. They were counterbalanced by the great growth in television audiences—spurred by the televising of the Coronation in 1953 and by the spread of Independent Television in the mid-fifties, the viewing audience rose rapidly. By 1955 there were already an estimated 12,040,000 viewers, and their weekly patterns of 'looking in' are set out in Figure 10.

Although this meant that at the weekends, when the majority of plays were then televised, there was a potential audience of some five million people happy to watch the drama in their own homes, this new popular pastime did not have the same apparent impact upon 'straight' theatre attendances as it had upon the cinema and upon the once-popular radio drama. In the theatre it was *light* entertainment which lost its audience, and as variety theatres closed down over Britain, local authorities felt justified in encouraging the building of new post-war civic theatres for which it was felt—following the great initial success of Coventry's £250,000 Belgrade Theatre—there would always be an audience.

Certainly—as we intimated in the previous chapter—by 1960 the ruling elite of the West End would have also been justified in believing that they had weathered the coming of television, and that their future was reasonably secure. The post-war amateur boom, the growth of

167

educational drama and now the uprising of the new provincial repertory companies, all of which enjoyed some measure of public support, did not seem in the event to threaten the dominance of the national drama by the West End. Indeed the repertory companies seemed in the early sixties ready enough to regard transfer of their best shows to the West End as the ultimate accolade. In 1961 transfers included the Nottingham Playhouse production of Keith Waterhouse and Willis Hall's *Celebration* to the Duchess Theatre, the Oxford Playhouse production of *Hamlet* at the Strand, the Cambridge Arts Theatre Trust's production of Henry Chapman's *That's Us*, and the usual transfers to the West End from the Royal Court and Stratford East theatres.

There were perhaps, at the beginning of the 1960s, three signs only of substantial opposition to the pervasive West End style. The first was in the success of the Theatre Workshop at Stratford East which created, at its best, a style of performance that drew on older stage techniques than those created by the Victorian and Edwardian stylists, and a management that operated more on shared responsibility than upon the feudal systems established in the majority of professional theatre. There was in their work a rough nervous energy that was the antithesis of the languid posturing that had become the prevailing high style—and indeed, when Coward saw the Stratford East production of *The Hostage*, he paid unwitting tribute to its arresting novelty by abusing it as strongly as he knew how, and calling it 'amateur'. [2]

The second sign of genuine opposition to West End dominance lay in Arnold Wesker's *Centre 42*, a movement named after the number of the resolution in which, for the first time, the Trades Union Congress had agreed to support the arts, and a movement which enjoyed a brief life in the early sixties. Its aims were to take music, literature and drama direct to those majority groups which had no contact with the best things, and to present them simply, in non-artistic locations. Noel Coward's reaction, when Wesker called upon him to recruit him to the cause, sufficiently indicates the gulf that still existed between Wesker's kind of populism and West End thinking:

> 'Last week Arnold Wesker, much to my astonishment, telephoned from London to say he wanted to come and see me! I invited him immediately, devoured by curiosity. He arrived looking grubby and peculiar in drab colours and his wife's sweater, which was definitely a mistake either for her or for him. It turns out he wants me either to donate money or to give a preview of *Sail Away*

168

in order to raise funds for 'Centre 42', a Labour-promoted scheme for bringing culture to the masses. They propose to organise Festivals all over green England which will include plays (unspecified) in the round, little exhibitions of modern painting and sculpture, merry folk singing and dancing, etc. This is all designed to wean the workers away from football pools, doggies and bingo and such wickedness, and teach them really to appreciate Henry Moore and Benjamin Britten and, at a pinch, me. The whole project, of course, sent me off into dreadful giggles, from which I later recovered and gave him a sharp talking-to about wasting his talent and energy on an already-gained cause and an old-fashioned one at that. I refused absolutely to contribute a penny or even a thought to such a lamentable waste of time.' [3]

Although *Centre 42* collapsed, it was arguably the forerunner of the late sixties growth of a new 'alternative' theatre, a loosely knit amalgam composed largely of small-scale touring drama groups who shared something of the objectives of Wesker's pioneering unit. Some ten years later the 'alternative' movement was a significant item in Arts Council funding, in numbers if not in monetary total. The 1974/75 figures for England only were then as follows:

	No. of companies	Money given	% of total
'National' companies	2	£1,793,750	55%
Repertory and Co.	61	£1,190,407	37%
'Alternative' theatre	80	£270,993	8%

In the early part of the seventies there was indeed a feeling that the movement represented something of a significant threat to the West End. It was not only numerically significant, but there was success reported in developing new popular styles, and in finding responsive audiences in untheatrical and new locations. It even established 'alternative' venues within establishment territory; as Jim Hiley said in *Time Out* (25th October 1973), 'Several defiantly 'Fringe' policies function much closer to Piccadilly Circus than a number of West End operations.' Other companies away from London claimed some success both in reviving popular theatre forms and in finding new audiences, particularly the 7:84 company, whose work has been lucidly discussed by their playwright/director John McGrath. [4]

In broad terms however the 'challenge' from the alternative movement weakened after the mid-seventies. A 1976 report revealed that their audiences were small, and every bit as well educated and highly privileged as audiences for the theatre with which they had seemed to be in opposition[5]. Many of the well-established groups, reasonably enough, lost their appetite for touring and innovation and looked for the safety and comfort of a permanent home[6]. Observers noticed that the subsidy per audience member was in many cases even higher than that given to the establishment theatres, and that far from breaking new ground, the 'alternative' companies were settling into ruts as safe and as comfortable as those made by the supposed opposition. As the West End managers had done, they joined together to advertise and the collected newspaper advertisements for 'Alternative Theatre' became as familiar in some newspapers as advertisements for the 'West End' had been, in Edwardian England, in others. They developed, through the Arts Council, a touring grid which set off the favoured companies on provincial routes as well-trodden in their way, as were the routes between provincial theatres for the 'West End companies' before the First World War. With some exceptions, the general message of their dramas was as predictably left wing and didactic as their West End forebears' had been conservative and bland. By the early eighties it was hard to see the movement creating any kind of new popular theatre, and the essential problem remained, in Michael Billington's phrase, the lack of work in the British theatre 'capable of addressing large numbers of people simultaneously.' [7]

A third form of opposition to the West End's dominance had been created by 1960 from a most unexpected quarter. In 1960 a new theatre, founded expressly upon the belief that the proscenium arch conventions were exhausted and that the centre of theatrical interest should be moved away from St Martin's Lane, opened. It was called the Mermaid, and it opened, surprisingly, within the confines of the ancient City of London itself.

For the historian who knows something of the long record of ill-feeling between the professional theatre and the governors of the City, Bernard Miles' achievement in gaining support from the City fathers for such a venture will be obvious enough. For opposition to theatre was deep-rooted. In 1594 the City's Lord Mayor wrote to the Lord High Treasurer to protest that plays at the new Swan theatre were 'nothing else but unchaste fables, lascivious devices, shifts and cozenage, and matters of like sort.' Three years later another Mayoral letter listed four major objections to plays and playhouses. They corrupted youth, attracted vagrants, encouraged sloth in servants, and bred general infection.

Faced with such powerful hostility, the public playhouses were actually driven from the precincts of the City long before Cromwell closed all playhouses in 1642. And when the theatre was 'restored', some eighteen years later, the City contained no playhouse, and indeed there are few records of any performances there until the Mermaid came to be built. Its general hostility to the 'unchaste fables' of the drama was one reason why the capital's playhouses were never built in anything like an even spread throughout the centre of London.' [8]

When Miles formed his Mermaid theatre, in the early fifties, it was not with any intention of breaching this citadel. The first Mermaid productions in fact were given in a converted schoolroom at the rear of the Miles' house in St. John's Wood. They were however already performances of interest to a student of theatre management, for in converting and staffing that small and somewhat improvised theatre Miles departed radically from well-established practice. First, the traditional 'rights' of the various backstage professionals, together with their attendant demarcation lines, were ignored. In Peter Daubeny's words:

> 'One of the charming elements about those intense preparations was the almost complete absence of the specialist. People tried their hand at task after task they had never tackled before— distempering, whitewashing, painting, floor laying. In this age, when every trade is jealously circumscribed, you might have thought such antics would have aroused the contempt, if not the disapproval, of the two professional builders who were busy on the more complicated structural alterations. Not a bit of it. They gave us much help and advice.' [9]

Second, he ignored the usual patterns of artists' payment, urging artists to work for the cause rather than for commerce, and achieving the spectacular coup of having Kirsten Flagstad sing twenty performances of Dido in *Dido and Aeneas* for two pints of oatmeal stout a day. At the other end of the scale of celebrity, a boy from the local Grammar School, Terry Wade, played Ariel alongside Miles' Caliban in *The Tempest*.

It was however the general philosophy of the Mermaid more than its unconventional methods of employment and working which showed that it contained within itself at least the germs of a revival of a form of popular theatre. It was begun in the belief that a simpler style of staging and production were now necessary, and that producers had, 'said all

In the early eighties up to twelve major theatres were dark at any one time.

that can be said inside the picture frame'. They looked for a larger venue to meet a larger audience, after the success of their cramped St. John's Wood season, and, when the Coronation of Queen Elizabeth II was imminent, had the temerity to approach the Gresham Committee in the City to ask whether they could present a season within the Royal Exchange itself. To their surprise, permission was granted; the season was successful and the Mermaid directors were then able to gain widespread City help to convert the old warehouse in Puddle Dock into the Mermaid theatre. It opened in 1960. Miles expressed the hope that it would 'enable the Theatre to take root in the City, and so help shift the emphasis from St Martin's Lane and Leicester Square a little more Eastward Ho.' [10]

However neither Bernard Miles nor anyone else possessed of ordinary mortal foresight could have foreseen the astonishing changes that were to take place over the next decades. For in 1960, neither the National Theatre nor the Barbican Arts Centre were being discussed in anything like their ultimate form. There was a Barbican Committee which had come into being in 1952—following the success of the Festival of Britain in revitalising the bombed and derelict South Bank of the Thames in 1951, it was felt some similar enterprise was needed to restore the bombed city area north of St. Paul's. The committee was concerned above all to recreate the city as a genuine centre of population—even before the wartime bombing the population had been steadily declining, and in 1951 it had dropped from its 1851 level of 160,000 to fewer than 10,000 inhabitants. They were discussing at the time therefore a species of new town, with the City schools in its centre, and with limited performance spaces for the schools and for the residents. Until 1964 the possibility of there being any kind of professional theatre company in residence there was not even considered.

Nor were there, in 1960, signs that the long-discussed National Theatre might one day become a concrete reality. The theatrical gossip was that the likeliest national company would emerge from a merger of the Shakespeare Memorial Company (which had just gambled on their future by moving to a London base at the Aldwych theatre) and the Old Vic company. The conventional wisdom was certainly that London could only complement its West End theatre by one large subsidised theatre. The Shakespeare Memorial Company was warned that it could not expect subsidy and support upon a major scale.

However, in the early sixties, events moved with some speed. On the

12th July 1961 the government announced that £1,000,000 had been earmarked for the proposed National Theatre on the South Bank. Attempts to merge the Old Vic and the (by now) Royal Shakespeare Company foundered. The Barbican Committee, encouraged by the suggestion in the Arts Council's 1964 publication *Housing the Arts*, that it might house a kind of British 'off-Broadway' series of productions in its new theatre, began to think in bigger and more 'commercial' terms, and by 1965 the RSC management was investigating the possibility of becoming the Barbican's resident company[11]. Five years after the opening of the new Mermaid theatre therefore, two vast new state subsidised theatrical complexes were being discussed, and the Mermaid was no longer leading the centre of theatrical interest Eastward Ho.

Both the National Theatre and the Barbican Arts Centre have had their development extensively researched [12] and there is no point in doing more here than reminding ourselves of their development. The National Theatre opened in its new building in 1976, and the Barbican theatres were opened in 1982. The cost of each project was vastly in excess of initial budgets—the National theatre building cost more than £11,000,000 and the whole Barbican complex cost a staggering £184,000,000. Although both theatre complexes were expensively equipped, both suffered from humiliating technical failings—the National theatre's expensive revolve never worked satisfactorily, and the actors found backstage conditions at the Barbican nearly impossible, as they were working in airless chambers without adequate air-conditioning. In spite of earlier threats both companies received vast state aid for their work; in 1983 it was announced that the 83/4 grant in aid to the National theatre company would be £6,390,000, and for the entirety of the RSC's activities, £3,600,000, (the two totalling rather less than the £10,445,000 promised to the nation's ultimate symbol of Glory, the Royal Opera House).

Naturally, the two great state organisations changed the theatrical map of London more completely than it had been changed for a century. A visitor could now readily observe that although the 'alternative' theatre had made little difference to the West End—indeed, one West End manager, Ian Albery, had begun the practice of bringing 'alternative' shows into the West End—the two great state companies had most assuredly done so. For though attendances at the National's three theatres, and the Barbican's two, were high, an average of some six older theatres were always standing unused in London's centre. In the crudest business terms, had their ten million pounds subsidy been directly available to producing companies aiming to use the *existing* West End theatres, they would have been open, and playing at acceptably low box-office prices. As however, a mixture of idealism, short-sighted intrigue and historical chance had decreed that London's theatrical life should once again be dominated by two large quasi-state organisations, it would seem to a disinterested observer that the state was, in effect, bribing a large segment of the former West End audience to desert, and to attend those buildings now decreed to be 'centres of excellence'.

We can at this stage give only a partial answer to the question of what kind of 'excellence' is being so expensively bought by the creation of the two great state houses. Certainly, their supporters would wish to say that they are justified in existing, and justified in offering competition to the existing West End theatre, because they offer work that is distinctive and good, and because they are enabled to be much more populist than their West End counterparts. When the National opened, it promoted a nationwide poster campaign proclaiming 'The National Theatre is Yours', and when the Barbican Arts Centre opened, a somewhat tired and emotional City Father assured television viewers that the Barbican was the City's gift 'to the nation'.

Yet in the simplest sense of the term, the two organisations *cannot* be popular. The average number of seats in each of their five auditoria is a little over 900, which means that a tag phrase such as 'The National Theatre is Yours' belongs to that small class of statements which become manifestly untrue as soon as the majority are persuaded to believe them. The marketing strategies of both companies have to be concerned not so much with the finding of a vast new popular audience, as with the segregating and organising of their existing one. Even if the majority of Londoners were to believe that the Barbican is a gift to the common people, they have to face the fact that were they seized by a general desire to visit the smaller of the Barbican's two theatres—called, with unwitting irony, 'The Pit'—and if the establishment were willing to continue the subsidy of between £15 and £18 a seat for such a period, [13] it would take more than 75 years for a majority of persons living within the GLC area to get a seat. In a simple sense, it is therefore true to say that by their very natures the two organisations cannot pursue a policy which is populist.

Which leaves us with the argument over 'centres of excellence'. That says that the state is justified in distorting the theatre market, not

175

because it is necessary to counteract the existing distortion created by the West End managers and all their influences, but because they will become 'centres' of a kind of theatre which, good in itself, also acts as a lever to all standards within the profession. Thus the heirs of Binkie Beaumont will find their sights raised, their styles of management mysteriously elevated by the very existence of the National and the Barbican.

Again, it is hard to see how such an argument can hold up. For in so many ways, and certainly in their staffing and conspicuous consumption, the two state companies seem to be the natural heirs of Tennent Productions Limited rather than of any other kind of theatre. They are, first, irrevocably London companies. Second, they seem to many observers to be overstaffed—although their staffing patterns vary, their combined staff numbers total some 1,550—and complaints of overspending are so rife that in December 1982 the Minister for the Arts let it be known there was to be an investigation into allegations of overspending by the national companies. Third, although their technical values are high, as were Tennent's, there is often reason to doubt whether the object of such expensive care is quite the right one; the cult shows of the two companies are at the time of writing two lavish musicals, *Poppy* at the Barbican, and *Guys and Dolls*, at the National. And when the National company shows that it is 'ours' by touring, its productions, from Somerset Maugham to Oscar Wilde, seem to many of the provincial managers to be oddly reminiscent of Tennent's, except that they are, of course, very much more expensive to take in.

In other words there must be more than a suspicion that the populist and the 'centre of excellence' argument are neither finally very convincing. In so many respects the two state companies seem to belong quite naturally to the old West End traditions of 'good' theatre practice—the managers of both companies sit on the board of SWET— but with the essential difference that each receives massive state subsidy. A pessimistic view therefore is that as the consenting theatre audience, willing to adhere to the Edwardian notions of theatre even when housed in new concrete buildings, slowly dwindles in size, so the RSC and the National will be the survivors, not because they *competed* with the nature of theatre created by the West End managers, but because they are the only segments of West End theatre that can continue to meet even that audience's expectations. Such a view is not a novel one, as *The Stage* glumly reported on 22nd July 1982:

176

'Sir Peter Hall, speaking at a lunch given by the London Tourist Board last week, sounded a gloomy note of which we would do well to take heed. Noting that more London theatres than ever before were closed—a circumstance that is particularly ominous considering that this is supposed to be the height of the tourist season—he forecast that by the start of the next decade London theatre would consist of the National and the RSC, always provided that they received sufficient cash, and a few musicals. The commercial theatre was in fact in danger of dwindling away altogether—unless.

Unless, one school of thought would have us believe, we prop up the theatre with more and more public money, which, quite honestly, we don't think we are going to get. Unless, say others, the theatre is made more accessible, hence the proliferation of computerised box-office and marketing schemes. All excellent in their way, but not much use if people prefer to do something else anyway.'

The 'something else' which people prefer to do may well, it is important to remind ourselves, be a different form of theatre. The dwindling audience for West End, and West End-related, theatre does not mean that we have decided *en bloc* to eschew all forms of the drama. It is true that fewer than 2% of the population of London now seem to go to their theatres; [14] as against the 13% in the age of the first Elizabeth, but many more than 14% enjoy televised drama weekly, and great crowds are drawn to those spectacles—the festivals, carnivals and fairs which still exist in the capital—which seem to demand less archaic ritual from their audience and offer so much more by way of vivid and immediate excitement. It is not true that Drama is dying; it is true that West End Theatre is.

Late in the day, and in spite of their tendency to blame everything except the social aspirations of their own forebears, there is evidence that some West End managers have recognised the need for change. Conspicuous consumption has lessened somewhat, and production costs are sometimes almost frugal—the long-running West End hit *No Sex Please We're British* was for instance staged by John Gale for the modest sum of £12,000. For the first time in the late seventies the managers began, collectively, to undertake proper market research (some first results of which are summarised in Appendix IV), and some managers, notably Ian Albery, began to use their prime locations to attract lunchtime and other audiences, so that theatres did not stand idle during the daytime. They began to instal equipment which, it was hoped, might enable ordinary people to book without embarking upon the ancient and elaborate Edwardian rituals, and they began the practice of selling at half-price a few of the unsold, expensive, seats for performances that would otherwise have been half empty.

The question must be asked however whether a much more dramatic change is not needed than these few managerial shifts would seem to offer. Perhaps nothing less than a total change in our concept of theatre will be satisfactory. To try to re-jig the nature of theatre in our present context leaves us suspended like the Arts Council—by 1981/82 the Council had *slightly* reduced the total amount given to the national companies (to 45.9%) and *slightly* increased what was given to the alternative companies (15.4%), but as a large number of experimental small scale productions were in fact mounted by the national companies and as the alternative companies appeared in many establishment venues, including the West End itself, it hardly seemed a shift of great moment. There was still no move to find again a theatre that could simultaneously address large numbers of people, nor any move to widen our concept of drama to include the discarded world of popular entertainment, or the submerged world of genuine community drama— in which folk were encouraged to enjoy guiltlessly the pleasures of the dramatic charade, the summer carnival or the well-told tale.

For it is likely that even such forthright warnings as that given by Sir Peter Hall and discussed above do not trouble the consciences of the many. And for good reason. They know that in spite of the attempts to equate the two the dramatic life of a nation is not finally to be judged by its willingness to support one form of establishment theatre, and even if every London theatre were to collapse, the majority know, if they give any thought to the matter at all, that it will make little difference to the quality of their lives. The amateur drama, the story-telling, the media entertainment, the festivals will all go on. What we term 'the West End' will disappear as 'the masque' disappeared, and indeed it will be seen, at the end, to have somewhat resembled the masque—an expensive entertainment which, though presented in the name of general improvement, was largely a pleasant distraction for the privileged, and which at the end became jaded, drab and unwanted.

It is certainly unlikely that additional 'investment', novel marketing schemes, or a re-thought 'presentation' will do anything to save the existing theatre— *unless we are prepared to re-think its central nature.* And there is daily, in our large quasi-state West End companies as well as in our long-established 'commercial' ones, depressing evidence that much in our theatre practice would be still comfortably familiar to Hare, Bancroft and Wyndham.

In spite of the veneer of modernity, West End managements are still spending too much on products which, however they are marketed, do not touch popular nerve. A chance look at the current issue of *The Stage* for example (20th January 1983) yields the front page news that, 'A major advance in computerised box-office technology is set to spark off another ticket selling revolution in Britain', and that a national computer network is going to link—at considerable expense—all theatre box-offices. Further down the same page is a report that the lush West End spectacular *Camelot*, which cost £600,000 to stage, had been re-directed at enormous additional expense by a director flown over from America. It was however still going to close because, in spite of the fact it boasted an expensive West End 'star', hired for his great drawing power, it was actually playing to 'minute' audiences! Sadly, in the juxtaposition of those two stories, can be read forms of mismanagement that go back a century and more and which still have their roots in simple Victorian snobbery.

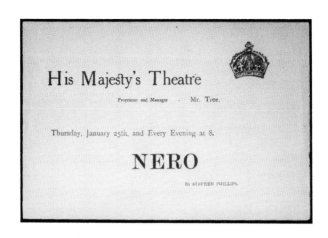

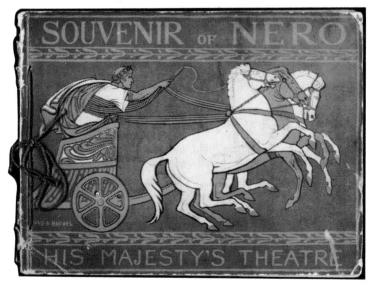

Beerbohm Tree had flimsy programmes for the gallery, rather more substantial ones (top) for the circle and stalls, and a special souvenir programme (bottom) priced at 1s or 1s 3d by post. None contained advertising. They remain as splendid momentoes of the West End at its height.

Appendix I
West End Theatres

The following were at some time during the period of the study considered to be West End theatres. In each case the last, or best-known name, is used for a theatre which has changed names during the period. The opening date is given if it was after 1840.

Name	Address	Former Names		Opening Date
Adelphi	409-412 Strand	1840	Theatre Royal	
		1867	Royal Adelphi Theatre	
		1901	Century	
		1902	Adelphi	
		1930	Royal Adelphi	
		1940 ff.	Adelphi	
Aldwych	Aldwych, Strand			1905
Alhambra Palace	27 Leicester Square	1854	Panoptican of Science and Art	1854
		1858	Alhambra Palace	
		1853	Royal Alhambra	
Ambassadors	Tower Street, Holborn			1913
Apollo	Shaftesbury Avenue			1901
Cambridge	Earlham Street, Holborn			1930
Coliseum	St. Martin's Lane			1904
Comedy	Panton Street, Westminster			1881
Covent Garden	Bow Street, Westminster	1847	Royal Italian Opera **and** Royal English Opera	
		1897	Royal Opera	
		1939	Royal Opera House	
Criterion	221 Piccadilly Circus			1874
Daly's	8 Cranbourn Street	**1937 ff.**	**Closed**	1893
Drury Lane	Catherine Street			
Duchess	Catherine Street			1929
Duke of York's	St. Martin's Lane	1892	Trafalgar Square Theatre	1892
		1894	Trafalgar Theatre	
		1895 ff.	Duke of York's	
Empire	Leicester Square	1849	Saville House	1849
		1856	Linwood Gallery	
		1862	El Dorado	
		1863	Criterion Music Hall	
		1869	Royal Denmark Theatre	
		1880	Royal London Panorama	
		1882	Pandora Theatre	
		1884	Empire Theatre	
		1924 ff.	**Cinema**	
Fortune	Russell Street, Covent Garden			1924
Gaiety	354 Strand	1862	Gaiety	1862
		1864	Strand Music Hall	
		1868	Gaiety	
		1903 ff.	**Closed**	
	Aldwych	**1950 ff.**	**Closed**	1903
Garrick	Charing Cross Road			1889
Globe	Newcastle Street, Strand	**1902 ff.**	**Closed**	1868
	Shaftesbury Avenue	1906	Hicks Theatre	1906
		1909 ff.	Globe	
Haymarket	7-8 Haymarket	1853	Haymarket Theatre	
		1855	Theatre Royal, Haymarket	

Name	Address	Former Names		Opening Date
Her Majesty's		1901 1952 ff.	His Majesty's Her Majesty's	
Hippodrome	Cranbourn Street			1900
Imperial	Tothill Street	**1907 ff.**	**Closed**	1876
Kingsway	Great Queen Street, Holborn	1882 1890 1894 1895 1907 **1941 ff.**	Novelty Theatre New Queen's Theatre Eden Palace of Varieties Novelty Theatre Kingsway Theatre **Closed**	1882
Little	John Adam Street, Adelphi	**1941 ff.**	**Closed**	1910
Lyceum	Wellington Street, Strand			
Lyric	29 Shaftesbury Avenue			1888
New	St. Martin's Lane			1903
New London	Drury Lane			
Olympic	6-10 Wych Street, Strand	1840 1853 1890 1893 **1904 ff.**	Olympic Pavilion Olympic New Olympic Olympic Music Hall **Closed**	
Opera Comique	299 Strand	**1899 ff.**	**Closed**	1870
Palace	Cambridge Circus	1891 **1893 ff.**	Royal English Opera **Palace**	1891
Palladium	Argyll Street	1871 1884 1910 ff.	Hengler's Grand Cirque National Skating Palace Palladium	1871
Phoenix	Charing Cross Road			1930
Piccadilly	Denman Street			1928
Playhouse	Northumberland Avenue	1882 1933 **1951 ff.**	Royal Avenue Playhouse **Closed**	1882
Prince Edward	Old Compton Street	1930 1978	Casino Prince Edward	1930
Prince of Wales's	Charlotte Street, St. Pancras	1840 1865 **1881 ff.**	Queen's (known as 'The Dust Hole') Prince of Wales's **Closed**	1884
Prince of Wales	Coventry Street, Piccadilly	1884 1886 ff.	Prince's Theatre Prince of Wales	1911
Prince's	Shaftesbury Avenue			1911
Princess's	73 Oxford Street	**1902 ff.**	**Closed**	1840
Queen's	Long Acre	**1879 ff.**	**Closed**	1850
Royalty	73 Dean Street	1840 1850 1870 **1938 ff.**	Royal Soho Theatre Soho Theatre Royalty **Closed**	1840
Royalty	Portugal Street			1960
St. James's	King Street	**1957 ff.**	**Closed**	1935
St. Martin's	West Street, Holborn			1916
Saville	135 Shaftesbury Avenue			1931
Savoy	Strand			1881
Scala	Charlotte Street, St. Pancras			1905
Shaftesbury	Shaftesbury Avenue	**1941 ff.**	**Closed**	1888
Strand	Aldwych	1905 1909 1911 1913 ff.	Waldorf Strand Whitney Theatre Strand	1905
Terry's	106 Strand	**1910 ff.**	**Closed**	1887
Toole's	King William Street	1854 1869 1876 1882 **1895 ff.**	Polygraphic Hall Charing Cross Theatre Folly Toole's **Closed**	1854
Vaudeville	404 Strand			1870

Name	Address	Former Names		Opening Date
Westminster	12 Palace Street			1931
Whitehall	Whitehall			1930
Winter Garden	Drury Lane	1840	Great Mogul	
		1851	Middlesex Music Hall	
		1919 ff.	Winter Garden	
Wyndham's	Charing Cross Road			1899

The two Barbican theatres, and the three auditoriums at the National theatre, the Olivier, Cottesloe and the Lyttleton, should now be added to the list.

Appendix II

Members of SWET, 1908, and Past Presidents

FOUNDER MEMBERS, 1908

President	Sir Charles Wyndham
Hon Members	Sir Squire Bancroft
	John Hare
Members	Beerbohm Tree
	Cyril Maude
	Edward Terry
	Fred Terry
	Lewis Waller
	George Edwardes
	J. Gatti
	Tom B. Davis
	Frank Curzon
	Otho Stuart
	A. Bourchier
	George Alexander
	Frederick Harrison
	Seymour Hicks
	A. Chidleigh
	William Greet
	J. E. Vedrenne
	A. Collins
	Chas Frohman
	Lena Ashwell
	Mrs D'Oyly Carte

PAST PRESIDENTS

1908 - 1910	Sir Charles Wyndham
1910 - 1912	Sir George Alexander
1912 - 1915	Sir Herbert Beerbohm Tree
1915 - 1920	J. M. Gatti
1920 - 1923	J. E. Vedrenne
1923 - 1941	Walter Payne

184

1941 - 1945	Sir Bronson Albery
1945 - 1949	Walter Payne
1949 - 1952	S. E. Linnit
1952 - 1953	Sir Bronson Albery
1953 - 1955	Prince Littler
1955 - 1956	S. E. Linnitt
1956 - 1958	Stephen Mitchell
1958 - 1961	Frederick Carter
1961 - 1962	Peter Saunders
1962 - 1964	Leslie A. Macdonnell
1964 - 1967	Sir Emile Littler
1967 - 1969	Peter Saunders
1969 - 1970	Sir Emile Littler
1970 - 1972	Toby Rowland
1972 - 1975	John Gale
1975 - 1977	David Conville
1977 - 1979	Ian B. Albery
1979 - 1982	Rupert Rhymes
1982 - 1983	David Conville
1983 -	Bob Swash

Appendix III

A Note on West End Seat Pricing

As we have seen, in the 1840s, London's most serious theatre, Sadler's Wells, drew a large part of its income from an auditorium that featured a very large, popular, pit. Its overall range of prices (Most expensive 3s., Least expensive, 6d.) was also low - partly because the London managements were still mindful of the 'Old Price' riots earlier in the century, and were reluctant to raise them. In its effect nevertheless, the pricing of the Sadler's Wells theatre might be called populist.

It is interesting to note the likely effects if such a policy had continued to be followed by West End theatres throughout the following century. If we posit an 'average wage' for the 1840s of 18s. a week for the lower-paid Londoner (the sum Phelps paid for his nightwatchman), then it is easily seen that in the 1840s such a person would require to spend some 17% of his weekly income to enter the most expensive part of Sadler's Wells theatre, and rather less than 3% to enter the least expensive part. If we then, taking the *Statist Price Index** as our indicator, calculate what London theatre prices would have subsequently been if they had taken Sadler's Wells' populist pricing as their natural level, and had merely fluctuated according to the *general* movement of prices in subsequent decades, and if moreover we calculate how the 'Nightwatchman's Wage' might have altered if it had changed according to the *general* movements in the Wage Index over those same decades, we can then see what proportion of such a wage *subsequently* would have been necessarily spent to get the cheapest or the most expensive seat at a London theatre. The situation is set out in the following table:

---

* See Mitchell, B.R., with Deane, P., *Abstract of British Historical Statistics* (Cambridge University Press). pp.474,475. The Statist Price Index, based on wholesale prices and the unit value of imports, is not of course ideal for our purposes, but it 'covers a period for which no other detailed series are yet available'. (p.466).

Cost of entering London Theatres, based on a projection of Sadler's Wells' 'Popular Pricing' Policy

Year	Statist Price Index	'Popular Pricing' (as in 1840s)		Wage Index	'Nightwatch- man's Wage'	Proportion of 'Nightwatchman's Wage' needed to enter	
		Most Expensive	Least Expensive			Most Expensive	Least Expensive
1840s	89	3s 0d	6d	100	18s	17.3%	2.9%
1850	77	2s 7d	5d	100	18s	14.4%	2.3%
1860	99	3s 4d	6½d	115	£1 0s 7d	16.2%	2.6%
1870	96	3s 3d	6½d	133	£1 3s 11d	13.6%	2.3%
1880	88	3s 0d	6d	145	£1 6s 1d	11.5%	1.9%
1890	72	2s 5½d	5d	165	£1 9s 8d	7.2%	1.4%
1900	75	2s 7d	5d	180	£1 12s 4d	8.0%	1.3%
1910	78	2s 8d	5d	171	£1 10s 10d	8.6%	1.4%
1920	251	8s 9d	1s 4d	194*	£1 14s 11d	17.0%	2.7%
1930	97	3s 4d	6½d	213	£1 18s 4d	8.7%	1.4%

*The calculation of 194 is for 1925, when the workforce had been demobilised, and something like 'normal' industrial conditions obtained.

The table shows that, had such notions of pricing continued to prevail in London theatre, the lower-paid Londoner would have found the theatre within his purchasing power, certainly up to the outbreak of the Second World War. However, if we turn once more to the Bancrofts' 1880 banishment of the pit, and to their promotion of the 10s. stall as the major element in the West End theatres' income, we see a different picture. The *expensive* seats now represent around a third, and sometimes more than a half, of such a lower-paid Londoner's wage, although until the Second World War, the cheapest seats continued to be, theoretically at least, accessible by price:

Cost of entering London Theatres, based on a projection of the Bancrofts' 1880 Haymarket 'Stalls' revolution

Year	Statist Price Index	'Stalls Pricing' following 1880s		Wage Index	'Nightwatch- man's Wage'	Proportion of Nightwatchman's Wage needed to enter	
		Most Expensive	Least Expensive			Most Expensive	Least Expensive
1880	88	10s	1s	145	£1 6s 1d	38.3%	3.8%
1890	72	8s 2d	10d	165	£1 9s 8d	27.5%	2.8%
1900	75	8s 6d	10d	180	£1 12s 4d	26.3%	2.6%
1910	78	8s 10d	10½d	171	£1 10s 10d	28.6%	2.8%
1920	251	£1 8s 5d	2s 9½d	194*	£1 14s 11d	56.3%	5.5%
1930	97	10s 11d	1s 1d	213	£1 18s 4d	28.9%	2.8%

* As before

187

It is since the Second World War that the *lower* prices in London's theatres have crept steadily upwards, until they are (as the Arts Council's Finance Director, Tony Field, has pointed out with some asperity) not only very few in number, but frequently forty, fifty or even sixty per cent of the 'top' price.

Not all London managers have been insensible to the way in which pricing has put theatres out of the reach of the poorer-paid. And occasionally, the discussion has interlocked with discussion over booking the cheaper parts. Arthur Bourchier, the Socialist owner of the Strand theatre (1925-6) was criticised in the *Sunday Worker* (14th March, 1926) not for his high prices, but for not making his gallery and his remaining 'pit' bookable. He responded by saying (21st March, 1926) that the way West End theatre was would mean that if the cheaper areas in his theatre did become bookable, they would simply be booked in advance by the wealthy and the workers wouldn't get in.

There have been other attempts to keep all theatre seats within the purchasing power of the poorly-paid, including several attempts to run 'season tickets' or 'subscription seasons'. Sir Frank Benson, for example, advertised his 1899 Lyceum Season in the *Daily Mail* (20th November, 1899):

> 'Season tickets will be issued entitling holders to a reserved seat for each of the eight plays on one day a week; and subscribers may select the Thursday, Friday, Saturday, Monday, Tuesday or Wednesday series as best suits their conveniences. Prices from £3.15s to £1 for the series of eight nights.'

Plainly the difficulty was that, although such an offer meant that each play could be viewed for 2s 6d from the cheapest seats, in order to take advantage of the offer, the £1 or the £3.15s had to be found at the same time - and £1 was at least 60% of an average wage!

Keeping down individual seat prices however involves two aspects of managerial policy which are antithetical to the nature of 'West End Theatre'. First, there must be an end to conspicuous consumption behind the curtain. Second, before it, there must be an auditorium which includes a large popular provision. Both were distinguishing elements of Lilian Baylis' Old Vic - a theatre which continued its 'popular' pricing policies well beyond her death in 1937. Both too were distinguishing elements of Newton's 'Shilling Theatre', which he founded in the Grand Theatre, Fulham, in 1933. The theatre held 1,000, ran twice-nightly, and - apart from its gallery, which was 6d. - every seat was 1/-. Thus the maximum possible income was some £480*. By keeping down costs, the theatre ran for a time in modest profit, thus:

Income (Weekly)	£	Expenditure (Weekly)	£
12 performances at		Salaries	100
at £40 maximum	480	Theatre Staff	40
		Rent	20
		Rates	5
		Printing and Advertising	30
		Royalties	20
		Lighting	10
		Production Expenses	25
			250
		Weekly Profit from full houses	230
	480		480

The figures are so radically different from those given earlier in the book for West End production expenses, and pricing, between the wars, as to suggest one is talking about a quite different commodity. But the figures also suggest that (had anyone had the means and the will) such a popular theatre *could* have worked anywhere in London, including its very centre.

---

* Figures quoted by Marshall, N. 1947, *The Other Theatre*. London: Lehmann. p.218.

Appendix IV

On the Size of the London Theatre Audience

In Figure 5 we identified 55 'major' theatres, West End and Suburban, which in 1900 were running a programme of 'straight' drama. Our definition of straight drama was as wide as it could be - excluding only music hall, variety, opera, circus and magic shows. An equally generous definition would allow that there were some fifty remaining after the first World War, and some forty-five after the second. Although it has suffered decline in popularity, the theatre has not apparently suffered the dramatic rise and fall of the national cinema circuits. And within theatre at large, the West End has remained, in spite of its occasional crises, remarkably resilient. 'Touring theatres', a term used again in the most general way, numbered around 225 after the First World War, around 100 after the Second, and now number no more than a dozen all told. Provincial repertory companies, of which *The Stage* listed 220 after the Second World War, now struggle for survival with fewer than a quarter of that number. London's suburban theatres can now be counted on the fingers of one hand. Yet, in spite of the 'dark' theatres, there are currently 35 recognisably 'West End' productions in London, a figure not all that dissimilar from the kind of picture presented after the First World War.

Yet for three reasons, it would be wrong to see the present picture as other than ominous. The first reason, with which we have sufficiently dealt, is that the overall effect of the West End's values upon British Theatre in general has been to harm and all but destroy a great deal of the *rest* of the national drama. The second reason is that for the 'West End' productions even to remain 'the same' relative to the increasing size of London's population, and relative to its much greater accessibility for visitors, the number of theatres and productions should have very much *increased*, and they have not. Third, the number 35 is itself deceptive - the list of shows of a 'West End' variety advertised and apparently 'current' does not mean what it meant twenty-five, fifty-five, or eighty-five years ago.

The second point may be simply amplified. By setting the number of seats available at live productions against the population of London, Professor Harbage (as we saw in Chapter One) was able to calculate that 13% of London's population went to the theatre every week, and that about 25% *could* have gone, in Shakespeare's lifetime. The calculation for the year 1900, based on available seats at active theatres, suggests that in any one week, some 10% of the population could have gone. In 1900:

Population of Greater London   -   6,500,000 (in round terms)
Nightly seats available   -   83,034
Weekly seats available (× 8)   -   664,272

So approximately 10% of the population of Greater London (650,000) could have gone to some form of straight theatre each week.

The proportion which could have visited a specifically *West End* theatre was of course much less, rather less than 5%, as the nightly seats available in the West End numbered only some 32,215. Much more important, even the most generous definition of 'West End' yields only the fact that, if they wished, only some 4% of Greater London's present population could now go to the West End theatre, and only just over 5% could go to *any* kind of theatre in London.

In recent years the Society of West End Theatre has (for the first time) commissioned market research. A first report, based on data supplied by NOP Market Research Limited, was published in 1981, and a second report, based on research undertaken by Caroline Gardiner of City University, was published in 1983. In spite of S.W.E.T.'s natural desire to put a brave face upon events, the results amplify the third point mentioned above - that even the number of apparently 'live' venues still operating within the orbit of the West End is deceptive.

The reports—taken in conjunction with various interim figures issued by S.W.E.T—suggest that about 28,000 people visit West End productions in London each evening. On the face of it this means that only around 1.7% of Greater Londoners visit the West End every week*, although the high incidence of tourists attending the London theatre would suggest that it is in fact a very much lower proportion than that. Disregarding their origins however, it is obvious even to the outsider

---

* The NOP Survey suggested that there are around 100,000 GLC residents who go 'to the theatre' at least once a month, and 1.3 million who go to the theatre at all.

that such a nightly attendance cannot sustain the numbers of shows that seem to be 'running', particularly as some 'hits' are known to be playing to full houses. The 28,000 people are in fact unevenly distributed; a handful of theatres are playing to capacity, the remainder running at average attendances of well below the *overall* average of West End attendances, some 60%. (Indeed closer examination of the 35 shows currently listed shows that three have not yet opened, and that 10 or more are limping along on attendances which average less than 50%.)

The signs of inevitable decline are plain enough. The habits of theatre presentation, by now ingrained so deeply that people will argue that 'the' theatre *must* be run in the way it is, and the small 'public' theatres, together mean that the cost of theatre-going will continue to rise. In spite of the massive grants given to the huge national organisations that are now a part of the West End structure, and in spite of other indirect subsidies (such as the Arts Council's generous help to the Theatre Investment Fund, which puts money into West End shows), theatre prices will continue to rise. Theatre-going, at least in its West End guise, will seem mummified and dull in comparison with more active popular pleasures, and in comparison with the more vivid pleasures the media provide - and audiences will continue to shrink as a marginal pleasure becomes more and more expensive. The irony lies in the fact that we continue to use a language which implies that nothing has changed since the Athenians built a theatre that would accommodate the entire citizen population of their largest city, and when a theatre public was *the* public. When the regular attenders at a city's theatre account for less than one per cent of a city's population, it seems perverse to call them a *public* at all. In like manner, in the sense that the Greeks used the word, it is hardly appropriate to call the rituals in our little playhouses *theatre*, when the stories, rituals and dramatic myths by which the majority of the population actually live come so plainly from another source.

Book List and Sources

Anyone interested in West End theatre is of course faced with an inexhaustible commentary upon the productions, the lives of the actors and their commentaries upon life in general. Records of the managerial ambitions—that is the actual aims of management, their methods of employment, their financial accounts and their methods of marketing— are rarely available *in toto*, but have to be pieced together from general reminiscences and from such first hand materials as may still exist in the archives. The following list is of publications that contain some valuable information to the researcher, but practically none of them is exclusively concerned with West End management. It is however kept as brief as possible, and where an author has written copiously, usually only the most valuable source is mentioned.

Primary Sources

Archer, Frank *An Actor's Notebooks* London: Stanley Paul. 1912.

Bancroft, Squire *Empty Chairs* London: Murray 1925.

Bancroft, Squire and Marie *On and Off the Stage* London: Bentley 1888.

Benson, Constance *Mainly Players* London: Thornton Butterworth 1926.

Burnard, Francis *Records and Reminiscences* 2 Vols. London: Methuen 1904.

Cochran, C.B. *Secrets of a Showman* London: Dent 1925.

Coward, Noel *Present Indicative* London: Heinemann 1937.

Coward, Noel *Diaries* (Payn and Morley, Ed.) Toronto: Little, Brown and Co. 1982.

Craig, E.G. *Index to the Story of my Days* London: Hilton 1957.

Dexter, W. (ed.) *The Unpublished Letters of Charles Dickens to Mark Lemon* London: Halton and Truscott Smith 1927.

Fitzgerald, Percy *The World Behind the Scenes* London: Chatto and Windus 1881.

Gielgud, John *Early Stages* London: Macmillan 1939.

Glover, G.H. *Jimmy Glover; His Book* London: Methuen 1911.

Guthrie, Tyrone *A Life in the Theatre* London: Hamish Hamilton 1959.

Hawtrey, Charles *The Truth At Last* London: Thornton Butterworth 1924.

Hibbert, H.G. *A Playgoer's Memories* London: Grant Richards 1920.

Hollingshead, John *Good Old Gaiety* London: Gaiety Theatre Co. 1903.

Holloway, D. *Playing the Empire* London: Harrap 1977.

Knight, J. *Theatrical Notes* London: Lawrence and Bullen 1893.

Leverton, W.H. *Through the Box Office Window* London: T. Werner Laurie 1932.

Moore, Eva *Exits and Entrances* London: Chapman and Hall 1928.

Martin-Harvey, John *Autobiography* London: Sampson Low.

Morley, J. *Journal of a London Playgoer* London: Routledge 1866.

Rolph, C.H. *London Particulars* Oxford: O.U.P. 1980.

Stoker, Bram *Personal Reminiscences of Henry Irving* London: Heinemann 1906.

Terriss, E. *Ellaine Terriss, By Herself* London: Cassell and Co. 1928.

Terry, Ellen *Ellen Terry's Memoirs* (Craig, E. and St. John C. Ed.) London: Gollancz 1933.

Vanbrugh, Irene *To Tell My Story* London: Hutchinson 1908.

Primary Reference

Roose Evans, James *London Theatre* London: Phaidon 1977.
(A concise, but well documented history of London theatre).

Howard, Diane *London Theatres and Music Halls* 1850-1950. London: The Library Association. 1970.
(Managers of, and lists of library material on, 910 of London's Theatres and Music Halls).

Mander, Raymond and Mitchenson, Joe *The Theatres of London* London: Hart Davis 1961.
(Location and Historical account of 41 West End theatres, 11 'outer ring' theatres, 5 club theatres and 7 'dark' West End theatres. Also includes, pp. 290-292, an alphabetical list of West End architects).

Peter Noble *British Theatre* London; British Yearbooks. 1946.
(Contains a biography of 721 producers and actors working on the post-war West End stage, and also, pp. 374-382 casts lists of outstanding London productions staged during the Second World War).

Offord, John *British Theatre Directory* Eastbourne; John Offord Publications.
(Contains full details of all London theatre buildings, stage equipment, management, etc. Contains also full list of current producing managements. *An Annual publication*).

Secondary Sources

Allen, J. *Theatre in Europe* Eastbourne: John Offord Publications 1981.

Allen, S. *Samuel Phelps and Sadler's Wells Theatre* Connecticut: Wesleyan University Press 1971.

Arliss, G. *On The Stage* London: John Murray 1928.

Baker, Henry B. *The London Stage; Its History and Tradition 1576-1888* 2 Vols. London: W.H. Allen and Co. 1889.

Baker, Michael *The Rise of the Victorian Actor* London: Croom Helm 1978.

Booth, Michael *Victorian Spectacular Theatre* London; Routledge and Kegan Paul 1981.

Boulton, William *The Amusements of Old London* 2 Vols. London: John Nimmo 1901.

Bunn, Alfred *The Stage. Both Before and Behind the Curtain* 3 Vols. London: Richard Bentley 1840.

Cole, J.W. *The Life and Theatrical Times of Charles Kean* London: Bentley 1859.

Cross, Gilbert B. *Next Week—East Lynne. Domestic Drama in Performance 1820-1874* Lewisburg; Bucknell University Press 1977.

Darbyshire, A. *The Art of the Victorian Stage: Notes and Recollections* London: Sherratt and Hughes 1907.

Daubeny, Peter *Stage by Stage* London: Murray 1952.

Disher, Maurice Wilson *Pleasures of London* London: Robert Hale 1950.

Doran, John *The Eminent Tragedian; William Charles Macready* Cambridge, Mass: Harvard University Press 1966.

Donaldson, Frances *The Actor Managers* Chicago: Henry Regnery 1970.

Elsom, John *Erotic Theatre* London: Secker and Warburg 1973.

Fleetwood, Frances *Conquest, The Story of a Theatre Family* London: W.H. Allen 1953.

Godfrey, Philip *Back-Stage* London: Harrap 1933.

Hayman Ronald *The Set-up. An Anatomy of Theatre Today* London: Eyre Methuen 1973.

Hudson, Lynton *The English Stage, 1850-1950* London: Harrap 1951.

Landstone, Charles *Off-Stage* London: Elek 1953.

Lesley, Cole *The Life of Noel Coward* London: Penguin 1978.

Macqueen-Pope, W. *Ivor, The Story of an Achievement* London: Hutchinson 1951.

Macqueen-Pope, W. *An Indiscreet Guide to Theatreland* London: Muse Arts Ltd. Undated.

Maude, Cyril *The Haymarket Theatre* London: Grant Richards 1903.

McKechnie, Samuel *Popular Entertainments Through the Ages* London: Sampson Low 1936.

Meisel, Martin *Shaw and the Nineteenth Century Theatre* New Jersey: Princeton University Press 1963.

Nicholson, Watson *The Struggle for a Free Stage in London* Boston: Houghton Mifflin 1906.

Pearson, Hesketh *The Last Actor Managers* London: Methuen 1950.

Pemberton, Thomas *Charles Dickens and the Stage* London: George Redway 1888.

Priestley, J.B. *Theatre Outlook* London: Nicholson and Watson 1947.

Rowell, George *The Victorian Theatre* London: Oxford University Press 1956.

Scott, Clement *From 'The Bells' to 'King Arthur', A Critical Record* London: MacQueen 1896.

Scott, Constance *Old Days in Bohemian London* London: Hutchinson and Co. 1919.

Sherek, Henry *Not In Front of the Children* London: Heinemann 1959.

Sherson, Errol *London's Lost Theatres of the Nineteenth Century* London: John Lane, The Bodley Head 1925.

Short, E. and Compton Rickett, A. *Ring Up The Curtain* London: Herbert Jenkins 1938.

Stirling, Edward. Old Drury Lane *Fifty Years' Recollections of Author, Actor, Manager* 2 Vols. London: Chatto and Windus 1881.

Taylor, John R. *Rise and Fall of the Well-Made Play* New York; Hill and Wang 1967.

Trewin, John C. *Mr. Macready—A Nineteenth-century Tragedian and His Theatre* London: Harrap 1955.

Tynan, K. *Tynan on Theatre* London: Pelican 1964.

Wilson, A.E. *The Lyceum* London: Dennis Yates 1952.

Wyndham, Horace *Nights in London* London: The Bodley Head 1925.

State Support for the Theatre

Elsom, J. and Tomlin, N. *The History of the National Theatre* London: Jonathan Cape 1978.

Evans, I. and Glasgow, M. *The Arts in England* London; Falcon Press 1949.

Hutchison, R. *The Politics of the Arts Council* London: Sinclair Browne 1982.

Minihan, Janet *The Nationalisation of Culture* London; Hamish Hamilton 1977.

Pick, J. (ed.) *The State and the Arts* Eastbourne; John Offord Publications (City Arts) 1980.

Priestley, J.B. *The Arts Under Socialism* London: Turnstile Press 1947.

Articles and Journals containing Primary Source Material

The Era 1840-1939.

The Theatre 1877-1897.

The Stage 1881-1960.

Theatre World 1925-1960.

St. James Gazette 1885 10th Jan. - 27th Feb.
(6 articles on The Theatre Business).

The Builder General articles 1858-1922.

The Music Hall and Theatre Review London 1889-1912.

London Entr'acte 1869-1907.

The Theatrical Journal 1840-1873.

Locations of some Primary Source Material

Covent Garden Theatre Records of Covent Garden.

Bristol University Drama Department Library Beerbohm Tree Collection.

City University Arts Administration Department Resources Centre Video interviews with Cyril Mills, Dennis Martin (Players Theatre), Harry Tate Jr. (Music Hall), Doris Waters (E.N.S.A. and Variety), Etc., Radio Interviews.

Enthoven Collection, V and A Museum Lease of Box in Pit Tier to H. Vane by B. Lumley. Covent Garden 1846.
Coutt's receipts for Charles Kean's Salary. Haymarket 1848.
Articles of Agreement, Theatre Royal, Drury Lane 1812-1866.
Copyright Agreement; Vandenhoff 1866.

Agreement; Globe Theatre. Augustus Harris 1883.
Licence granted by Pigott. Grand, Islington 1883.
Agreement, Britannia Theatre. Sara Lane 1888.
Ledger of payments to performers. Alhambra Theatre 1898-1900.
Assignment of Lyceum to Irving, by Bateman 1878.
Account Books. Lyceum. Bram Stoker.
Documents relating to ownership of O'Toole's theatre 1893-1894.
Macready's Account Book. Drury Lane 1841-1843.
Accounts. Terry's Theatre 1904.
Accounts. Vaudeville Theatre 1904, together with Daily Returns.

Manuscript Room, British Museum A large and growing twentieth century collection.
Theatrical Collection, by J. Winston (38607).
Letters of John Hare 1844 ff (uncat.).
List of performances at various London theatres—1878 (39863).
Letters from Squire Bancroft (16926).
Letters to Sir Robert Peel, incl. letter from Dramatic Authors Society (40523/40526).
Letters, A. Pinero (45294).

Department of Print and Drawings, British Museum Architects plans of London theatres. Ephemera on Daly's, Globe, Wyndham's, St. James's.

Department of Printed Books, British Museum Comprehensive collection of scrapbooks, posters, pamphlets and monographs relating to London theatre.

Harvard University Library Family papers of Ben Webster, London Manager.

Henry Huntingdon Library, San Mariad, California 308 letters to John Hollingshead.

Folger Library, Washington Charles Kean Collection, incl. Charles Kean Receipt Book 1848.

Ohio State University Extensive collection of ephemera on nineteenth century London theatre.

Finsbury Library, St. John's Road, London Extensive collection of material relating to Sadler's Wells.

St. Marylebone District Library, Marylebone Road, London Ephemera relating to several theatres but particularly Princess's Theatre.

Hampstead Library, Swiss Cottage, London Material primarily relating to Scala theatre.

Guildhall Library, Basinghall Street, London Extensive collection of material relating to many central London theatres.

Mander and Mitchenson Theatre Collection Extensive collection of photographic material, playbills, programmes, etc. etc. Presently housed at 5 Venmer Road, Sydenham, but shortly to be moved.

Notes and References

1 Mismanagement and Snobbery

[1] Harbage, A. 1941. *Shakespeare's Audience.* Columbia: Columbia University Press. pp. 19-53.

[2] See Nicholson, W. 1906. *The Struggle for a Free Stage in London.* Boston: Houghton Mifflin.

[3] Anon. 1702. *Comparison Between the Two Stages.*

[4] See Baumol, W.J. and Bowen W.G. 1966. *Performing Arts—The Economic Dilemma,* Cambridge, Mass. and New York: M.I.T. Press and Twentieth Century Fund.

[5] Pinero, A. 1898. Letter to Frank Archer. In the Manuscript Collection, British Museum.

[6] Baldry, H. 1981. *The Case for the Arts.* London: Secker and Warburg. p.10.

[7] Between 1950 and 1970, for instance, actors employed by producing theatres usually rose by 20%, *off*stage employees by 120%. See Pick J. (Ed.) *The State and the Arts* Eastbourne; John Offord Publications. pp. 90/91.

[8] Priestley, J.B. 1947. *Theatre Outlook.* London; Nicholson and Watson p.37.

[9] Catty, J. 1982. 'West End Crisis'. *Drama; Quarterly Theatre Review.* Winter 1982.

[10] Calculations are based on the figures given in Howard, D. 1970. *London Theatres and Music Halls 1850-1950* [London: The Library Association]. And in *The Era* [1838-1939. London]. The 1960 calculation is based on the figures given in *The London Theatre Guide* [1960. London: Sphere Handbook], and elsewhere.

[11] Stoker, B. 1907. *Personal Reminiscences of Henry Irving* London: Heinemann. p.124.

[12] Sherek, H. 1959. *Not In Front of the Children* London: Heinemann. p.219.

[13] Daubeny, P. 1952. *Stage by Stage* London: John Murray. p.69.

[14] Braybrooke. 1825. *The Diaries of Samuel Pepys, 1660-1669* London. Entry for 8th December, 1668.

2 Popular London Theatre; 1840 and After

[1] 'Sketches from London Thoroughfares'. 8th January 1848. *Illustrated London News.*

[2]   *Dyos. 1961.* Victorian Suburb *Leicester; Leicester University Press. pp. 127-132.*

[3]   Cooney, E.W. 'The Origins of the Victorian Master Builders.' 1955 Vol. VIII *Economic History Review.*

[4]   Vanbrugh, Irene. 1948. *To Tell My Story* London: Hutchinson. p.45.

[5]   Cross, Gilbert B. 1977. *Next Week—East Lynne. Domestic Drama In Performance 1820-1874.* Lewisburg; Bucknell University Press. p.229.

[6]   Trevelyan, G.M. 1964. *English Social History [4].* London; Pelican. pp. 126, 127. The first Public Health Act of 1848 resulted in large measure from the work of Chadwick, then secretary to the Poor Law Commissioners.

[7]   'London's Air'. 3rd November 1849. *Illustrated London News.*

[8]   'The Great International Exhibition'. 11th January 1851. *Illustrated London News.*

[9]   Fleetwood, Frances. 1953. *Conquest—The Story of a Theatre Family.* London: W.H. Allen. p.69.

[10] Fawkes, R. 1979. *Dion Boucicault.* London; Quartet Books. p.41.

[11] 'Five Shilling Days and One Shilling Days'. 19th July 1851. *Illustrated London News.*

[12] 'London During the Great Exhibition'. 17th March 1851. *Illustrated London News.*

3 The Suburban Theatre and Samuel Phelps

[1]   Zwart, Peter. 1973. *Islington; A Guide.* London: Cassels.

[2]   'Report of the Managers of Sadler's Wells for the Diffusion of Shakespeareanity'. September, 1845. *Punch.*

[3]   Ibid.

[4]   'Pantomime'. 26th December 1845. *Illustrated London News.*

[5]   Allen, Shirley. 1971. *Samuel Phelps and Sadler's Wells Theatre.* Connecticut: Wesleyan University Press. p.83.

[6]   The bill is in the Sadler's Wells Collection at the Finsbury Library. It is also quoted in full in Professor Shirley Allen, *Op Cit.* pp.82-83.

[7]   'Sadler's Wells'. 28th February 1846. *The Times.*

[8]   Quoted in Zwart, P. *Op Cit.*

[9]   Dickens, Charles Jr. 1879. *A London Dictionary and Guide Book.* London: 26 Wellington Street.

[10] Burton J.G. (1819). *The Critic's Budget or A Peep Into the Amateur Green Room.* London: Onwhyn. The list is not complete.

[11] Phelps, W. May, and Forbes-Robertson, John 1886. *The Life and Life-Work of Samuel Phelps.* London: Methuen.

[12] Letter in Harvard Theatre Collection. No date. Headed 'Sunday Morn'.

4 The Refinement of the Bancrofts 1865-1885

[1] Hodder, E. 1901. *The Life of a Century.* London: George Newnes. pp.439-459.

[2] Donaldson, Frances. 1970. *The Actor Managers.* London: Weidenfeld and Nicholson. pp.17-45.

[3] Bancroft, Squire and Marie. 1911. *The Bancrofts; Recollections of Sixty Years.* London: Thomas Nelson and Sons. p.16.

[4] *Ibid.* pp.32-33.

[5] *Ibid.* p.80.

[6] Wilson Knight, G. 1962. *The Golden Labyrinth.* London: Methuen, University Paperbacks. p.303.

[7] Bancroft, Squire and Marie. *Op Cit.* p.97.

[8] *Ibid.* p.268.

[9] Ibid p.352. In shortened form the same comments appear in Bancroft, Squire. 1925. *Empty Chairs.* London; John Murray. pp.180-181.

[10] *Ibid.* p.265.

[11] *Ibid.* p.273.

[12] Quoted in full in Maude, Cyril. 1905. *The Haymarket Theatre.* London: Grant Richards. p.167.

[13] Bancroft, Squire and Marie. *Op Cit.* p.281.

[14] *The Theatre* March, 1880. 3rd Series. No. 3. p.130.

[15] *Ibid.* p.139.

[16] James, Henry. 1947. *The Scenic Art.* (ed. Allan Wade) New York: Hill and Wang Inc. p.136.

5 Entertainment in the West End

[1] *The Theatre.* September 1878. New Series. No. 2. p.102.

[2] Rowell, G. 1955. *The Victorian Theatre.* Oxford: The Clarendon Press. p.83.

[3] McKechnie, S. 1936. *Popular Entertainments Through the Ages.* London: Sampson Low. pp 140-141.

[4] Sims, G.R. 1888. *Ally Sloper's Half Holiday.* Quoted in Glasstone, V. 1975. *Victorian and Edwardian Theatres.* London: Thames and Hudson. p.54. With illustration.

[5] *The Century Magazine.* Vol. 35. November 1887 to April 1888. p.482.

[6] Gilbert, W. and Sullivan, A. 1881. *Patience.* Act 1.

[7] Hibbert, H.G. 1920. *A Playgoer's Memories.* London: Grant Richards. p.231.

[8] Hollingshead, John. 1903. *Good Old Gaiety.* London: Gaiety Theatre Company. p.8.

[9] *Ibid.* p.26.

[10] *Ibid.* p.77.

[11] Archer's Review of *King Lear,* 1892. See Irving, L. 1951. *Henry Irving, The Actor and his World.* London: Faber. pp.550-552.

6 The Tools of Management

[1] Trewin, J.C. (ed). 1967. *The Journal of William Charles Macready.* London: Longmans. pp.87-167.

[2] Wilson, G. 'Charles Kean; A Financial Report.' Richards, K. and Thomson, P. (eds.) 1971. *Nineteenth Century British Theatre.* London: Methuen. pp.39-50.

[3] See the description of the enterprise in Fawkes, R. 1979. *Dion Boucicault.* London: Quartet Books. p.133 ff. Boucicault also tried, and failed, to introduce twenty rows of numbered, bookable, seats in 1862—another experiment that was before its time.

[4] Wording on the bottom of the original advertisement.

[5] Leverton, W.H. 1932. *Through the Box Office Window.* London: T. Werner Laurie. p.141.

[6] Hawtrey, Charles. 1924. *The Truth At Last.* London: Thornton Butterworth. pp.143-144.

[7] Leverton, W.H. *Op Cit.* p.26. Booking for the pit and gallery was not generally introduced in London until the 1920s, and not at the Haymarket until 1926. Leverton, p.137.

[8] Metcalf, P. 1972. *Victorian London.* London; David and Charles. p.64. In addition to sources mentioned in this chapter, an indication of the development of advertising by West End managers can be gained from the chapter in Hawtrey, *Op Cit.*, entitled 'New Modes of Advertising the Play' pp.133-147, and from the brief discussion of the installation of electric lighting displays in Hollingshead, *Op Cit.* p.41.

[9] Barnes, J.H., in *The Nineteenth Century*. Feb. 1908.

[10] Shaw, G.B., in *The Saturday Review*. 1st May 1897.

7 Henry Irving and the Art of Conspicuous Consumption

[1] *Illustrated London News*. 31st July 1858.

[2] Stoker, Bram. 1907. *Personal Reminiscences of Henry Irving*. London: Heinemann. p.18.

[3] Stoker, Bram. 'The Question of a National Theatre' in *The Nineteenth Century*. May 1908.

[4] Figures taken from Hughes, A. 'Henry Irving's Finances; the Lyceum Accounts 1878-1899' in *Nineteenth Century Theatre Research*. Vol. 1 No. 2. pp.79-87.

[5] Guthrie, T. 1959. *A Life in the Theatre*. London: Hamish Hamilton. pp.144-145. The play's opening night was followed by 'an enormous party', given by Binkie Beaumont. p.145.

[6] In his personal reminiscences of Irving Stoker devotes more than 20 pages to Irving's social links with Royal Academicians, and 10 pages to his socialising with Gladstone and with the Earl of Beaconsfield. By contrast his relationships with his own company are far less fully discussed, and several of the leading actors in Irving's company are not mentioned at all. For Irving's strange treatment of his fellow artists see Martin Harvey, John. (Undated) *Autobiography*. London: Sampson Low. p.91. After Irving's death the company were not permitted to pay their last respects and to view his corpse. p.53.

[7] Daubeny, P. 1952. *Stage by Stage*. London: Murray. p.55.

[8] Sherek, Henry. 1959. *Not In Front of the Children*. London; The Windmill Press. p.139.

[9] Fawkes, R. 1979. *Dion Boucicault*. London: Quartet Books. p.137.

[10] Stoker, Bram. *Op Cit*. pp.114-115. '. . . prolongued rehearsals mean a fearful addition to expense.'

[11] *Ibid*.

[12] Baxter, S. 1955. *First Nights and Footlights*. London: Hutchinson. p.37.

[13] The best description of the author's legal right in a dramatic work see McFarlane, 1980. *Copyright: the Development and Exercise of the Performing Right*. Eastbourne: John Offord Publications (City Arts).

[*14*] The full story is told by Burnard, F.C. 1904. *Records and Reminiscences.* London: Methuen. Vol. 2. p.372 ff. Authors' rights were finally safeguarded by the *Berne Convention on Authors' Rights 1886* and by the *Copyright Law U.S.A. 1891.*

[*15*] Stoker, Bram. *Op Cit.* p.326 and p.329.

8 The West End 1890-1914

[*1*] Wyndham, Horace. 1925. *Nights in London.* London; The Bodley Head.

[*2*] Rolph, C.H. 1980. *London Particulars.* Oxford: University Press. p.71.

[*3*] Chaplin, C. 1966. *My Autobiography.* London: Penguin. pp.17-28.

[*4*] Macqueen-Pope, W. 1947. *Carriages at Eleven.* London: Hutchinson. pp.10-11.

[*5*] At the turn of the century *The Stage* carried a regular report on the doings of the London Theatres' Masonic Lodge.

[*6*] Holloway, David. 1979. *Playing the Empire.* London: Harrap. p.56.

[*7*] James, Henry. 1947. *The Scenic Art.* (ed. Allan Wade). New York: Hill and Wang Inc. p.100.

[*8*] Replacing an earlier organisation, *The Provincial Theatre Managers' Association.* The records of TMA and SWET are kept at the headquarters of the two societies at Bedford Chambers, London.

[*9*] Thackeray, W.M. 1948. *The Book of Snobs.* London: 'He who meanly admires mean things is a snob.'

9 In Defence of Good Breeding 1918-1939

[*1*] Hibbert, H.G. 1920. *A Playgoer's Memories.* London: Grant Richards. p.219.

[*2*] Godfrey, P. 1933. *Backstage.* London: Harrap. pp.118-119.

[*3*] Of course a contributory factor in the theatre shortage was the great difficulty in building *new* theatres. Short, E. and Compton-Rickett, A. comment that, 'Moreover, at post-war costs, it was not profitable to build new theatres within 'the charmed circle . . . Something like £6,000 a year would have been asked for ground rent and another £40,000 would have been required for dispossessing existing tenants. These prime costs, together with

£100,000 for actual building, made £400 a fair return to a speculative builder of a West End theatre.' Only films and the most spectacularly profitable of stage shows could approach a weekly box-office income which could meet such a rental, and therefore speculators hardly ventured into theatre building at all. *Ring Up The Curtain*. London: Herbert Jenkins. p.250.

Godfrey, P. *Op Cit.* pp.131-132.

[4] *Ibid.* p.133.
[5] *Ibid.* p.121.
[6] Macqueen-Pope, W. 1951. *Ivor. The Story of An Achievement.*
[7] London: Hutchinson. p.300. Novello's earnings between the wars are listed on p.209.
[8] Quoted in Short, E. 1942. *Theatrical Cavalcade.* London: Eyre and Spottiswood. p.214.
[9] Hardwicke, Cedric. 1961. *A Victorian in Orbit.* London: Methuen. p.101.
[10] Kerr, F. 1930. *Recollections of a Defective Memory.* London: Thornton Butterworth. p.243.
[11] Gielgud, John. 1981. *An Actor and his Time.* London: Penguin. p.65.
[12] Guthrie, T. 1959. *A Life in the Theatre.* London: Hamish Hamilton. p.142.

10 The Rank and Snobbery of Sir Noel Coward

[1] *The Noel Coward Diaries.* (Ed. Graham Payn and Sheridan Morley). Boston: Little Brown and Company. Entry for 5th June 1957.
[2] *Ibid.* Entry for 19th September 1959.
[3] *Ibid.* Entry for 9th October 1960.
[4] *Ibid.* 5th December 1959.
[5] Lesley, Cole. 1978. *The Life of Noel Coward.* London: Penguin. p.203.
[6] *Diaries.* 25th October 1943.
[7] *Ibid.* 5th May 1945.
[8] *Ibid.* 31st December 1956.
[9] *Ibid.* 7th November 1954.
[10] W. Macqueen-Pope. *Op Cit.* p.21.
[11] Lesley, Cole. *Op Cit.* p.127.

[12] Quoted by Payn and Morley, in the introduction to the year 1959, in *The Noel Coward Diaries.* p.395.

[13] Tynan, K. 'A Tribute to Mr. Coward'. 1964. *Tynan on Theatre.* London: Pelican. p.288.

11 The Interval of the War

[1] Madge, C. and Harrisson, T. 1939. *Britain by Mass Observation.* London: Penguin. p.23 ff.

[2] Quoted in Fawkes, R. 1978. *Fighting for a Laugh.* London: Macdonald and Janes. p.12.

[3] Macqueen-Pope, W. Undated. *An Indiscreet Guide to Theatreland.* London: Muse Arts Ltd. p.44.

12 The West End in the Welfare State

[1] A video recording of Cyril Mills' recollections of the Olympia circus is in the Centre for Arts, City University.

[2] The West End managers however largely boycotted the great Post-War Theatre Conference, held in February 1948, and chaired by J.B. Priestley. They did not yet see *themselves* as a part of the general crisis in theatre, still less the instigators of the crisis.

[3] A result of the *National Parks and Access to the Countryside Act, 1949.*

[4] Marwick, A. 1982. *British Society Since 1945.* London: Penguin. p.34.

[5] Most public transport shut down early in the evening. So for visitors a trip to the West End theatre had either to be made by private car, or had to include the cost of overnight accommodation in London.

[6] Daubeny, Peter. 1952. *Stage by Stage.* London: Murray. p.35.

[7] *Ibid.* p.48.

[8] Priestley, J.B. 1947. *Theatre Outlook.* London: Nicholson and Watson. p.35.

[9] *Ibid.* p.6.

[10] In the period 1945-1960 the annual loss to Equity's membership was usually about two-thirds of the annual increase. Thus although Equity enrolled an average of 1,850 new members each year, the total membership had increased by the end of that period by only 9,000. For a full analysis see Hayman, R. 1973. *The Set-Up.* London: Eyre Methuen. pp.40-56.

[11] Alec Clunes successfully led the Arts Theatre company. Donald Wolfit periodically led his own company on major provincial tours.

[12] Drummond, J. 1947. *Playing to the Gods.* London: The Book Club.

[13] Sampson, A. 1962. *Anatomy of Britain.* London; Hodder and Stoughton.

[14] Hewison, R. 1981. *In Anger; Culture in the Cold War.* London: Weidenfeld and Nicholson. p.66.

[15] Tynan, K. 1964. *Tynan on Theatre.* London: Pelican. p.31.

[16] Baxter, B. 1955. *First Nights and Footlights.* London: Hutchinson. p.243.

[17] *Ibid.* p.247.

[18] Tynan, K. *Op Cit.* p.31.

[19] No popular movement had advocated its creation, and its formation had not been an aim of any of the parties contesting the first post-war election.

[20] See Leavis, F. 'Keynes, Lawrence and Cambridge' 1952. *The Common Pursuit.* London: Chatto and Windus.

[21] Drogheda. 1978. *Double Harness.* London: Weidenfeld and Nicholson. p.227.

[22] Priestley, J.B. *Op Cit.* pp.22-27.

[23] Evans, B. Ifor, and Glasgow, Mary. 1949. *The Arts in England.* London: Falcon Press. pp.85-86.

[24] Olivier, Laurence, 1946. Introduction to *British Theatre.* London: British Yearbooks. p.3.

[25] Priestley, J.B. *Op Cit.* pp.25/26.

13   The City and the Finale

[1] Taylor, G. 1976. *History of the Amateur Theatre.* Wiltshire: Venton. p.95.

[2] Diaries, 19th September 1959.

[3] Ibid. 16th January 1962.

[4] See McGrath, John. 1981. *A Good Night Out.* Cambridge.

[5] Gallup, 1976. The best case for the movement is Itzin, Catherine. *Stages in the Revolution.* London: Eyre Methuen. 1980.

[6] Pick, J. 1981. *Report on the Colloquy on Fostering Artistic Creation.* Strasbourg; Council of Europe.

[7] *The Guardian.* 28th December 1982.

[8] There was a small theatre known as 'The City Theatre' which briefly existed in Chapel Street in the early nineteenth century.

And the scholar William Poel was given permission to present a performance by the Elizabethan Stage Society at the Mansion House in 1897.

[9] Daubeny, Peter. 1952. *Stage by Stage.* London: John Murray. pp.117/118.

[10] Miles, Bernard. 1953. *The Mermaid; Performances and Prospects.* London: Mermaid Theatre.

[11] In addition to investigating many other possibilities. Almost as soon as the company arrived at the Aldwych, Peter Hall announced the theatre was inadequate.

[12] The most exhaustive account of the National Theatre is Elsom, J. and Tomalin, N. 1978. *The History of the National Theatre.* London: Jonathon Cape. The fullest account of the Barbican is by Boughton, D. *The Barbican Arts Centre.* Unpublished Ph.D. Thesis, City University.

[13] Critics of the City building schemes estimated just before its opening that building costs, and the attendant debt charges, amounted to a subsidy of between £14 and £17 a seat, paid for from the City rates. The RSC's Arts Council's grant to it for 1982/83, roughly divided, could be said to give the organisation some £5,000 a day attributable to their Barbican operation—thus, depending on the way the sum is done, an additional subsidy of between £1 and £3 a seat.

[14] The most recent calculation is that a total of eight and a half million attendances are made to the contemporary West End theatre each year.

Index

Titles are given in Italics

211

212

213

215